OTHER WORKS BY

Also by **Freydís Moon**
With a Vengeance
Exodus 20:3
Three Kings
Heart, Haunt, Havoc

Also by **Dorian Yosef Weber**
"Mizmor L'David" in *Changelings: An Autistic Trans Anthology*

Also by **Angela Sun**
"Love Letter at the Cusp of Exorcism" in *The Summer Gothic*
"Sea Song" and "Downtown" in *The Squawk Back*
"FIRST ACT OF A MOVIE WHERE I LOVED YOU THE ENTIRE TIME" in *Heavy Feather Review*

Also by **Tyler Battaglia**
"A House; A Haunting" in *The Summer Gothic*
"The Sixth Tree" in *Crow & Cross Keys*

Also by **Morgan Dante**
A Flame in the Night
Witch Soul

Also by **Cas Trudeau**
"(Hetero)trophic Love" in *The Summer Gothic*

Also by **Rafael Nicolás**
Angels Before Man

Also by **Quinton Li**
Tell Me How It Ends

DEVOUT
AN ANTHOLOGY OF ANGELS

DEVOUT
AN ANTHOLOGY OF ANGELS

Freydís Moon
Dorian Yosef Weber
Angela Sun
Ian Haramaki
Tyler Battaglia
Daniel Marie James
Morgan Dante
Cas Trudeau
Aurélio Loren
Rae Novotny
Rafael Nicolás
Emily Hoffman

Curated and edited by *Quinton Li*

DEVOUT: AN ANTHOLOGY OF ANGELS

Copyright © 2023 **Quinton Li**
Released August 29th 2023 by Quinton Li Editorial.

All rights reserved. No part of this anthology may be used or reproduced in any manner whatsoever without written permission, except in the case of brief quotations embodied in critical articles or reviews. Names, characters, businesses, organisations, places, events and incidents are either the product of the authors' imagination or are used fictitiously. Any resemblance to actual persons, living or dead, or locales is entirely coincidental.

Contact: Quinton Li (www.quintonli.com)
More information: https://devoutlogy.carrd.co/

Cover Artist and Layout Designer: **Alex Patrascu** (www.apatrascu.com)
Front Cover: "Angel with a Banderole" by Claude Mellan; The Metropolitan Museum of Art
Back Cover: "Sheet of Studies: Five Angels (recto)" by Giovanni Battista Tiepolo; The Metropolitan Museum of Art

The text in *Devout* is typeset in EB Garamond, and headers are set in Orpheus Pro.

ISBN: 978-0-6456815-6-7

EDITOR'S LETTER

Quinton Li

When there's ringing in my ears, I know there are angels around. Just as when I'm working away at a novel or any writing project, there's an angel behind me then, too.

I believe I was surrounded by a number of angels during the creation of *Devout: An Anthology of Angels*, from the angels in each story, to the angels watching over my shoulder, to every author who may or may not be an angel themselves.

Angels have always played an important part in my life, whether it's an image of safety and unconditional love, or the twisting, what we call, biblical depictions that make me feel things. Maybe I've seen an angel before, when I was too young to remember, or maybe I was an angel in a previous lifetime.

In any case, in this reality, I'm Quinton Li, the curator and editor of this anthology. I'm incredibly pleased to present this heart- and horror-felt collection by a group of writers and artists who love angels just as much as I do, maybe more!

Freydís, Dorian, Angela, Ian, Tyler, Daniel, Morgan, Cas, Aurélio, Rae, Rafael and Emily, you were all so wonderful to work with. You were passionate and excited, and that just motivated me even more to do my best for you. I'm grateful to have had this opportunity to curate my first anthology with you and I wish for many more cool projects between us.

Alex, there's no one else I'd rather work with to design this anthology. I might say this in every publication that we work together on, but I knew I wanted you to design and format this anthology from the start. Thank you for your hard work!

To every ARC reader who expressed interest in *Devout*, thank you! Your dedication to the authors in this anthology is inspiring and I'm so thankful for it!

And, of course, to every angel and angel lover reading this anthology. This is for you and I hope you find something familiar to curl up to, and something new to love.

Enjoy the *Devout Anthology*!

TABLE OF CONTENTS

VII	Editor's Letter † *Quinton Li*
3	The Angels at Harvest Church † *Freydís Moon*
9	I Know My Father † *Dorian Yosef Weber*
12	Seasons of God † *Angela Sun*
26	Resta Con Me † *Ian Haramaki*
42	Seraphim † *Ian Haramaki*
44	With Wings Like Madeleines † *Dorian Yosef Weber*
46	And The Mountains Melt Like Wax † *Tyler Battaglia*
58	The Mountains, The Mountains, The Mountains † *Tyler Battaglia*
60	We Suffer in Fire † *Tyler Battaglia*
63	Divine Body † *Daniel Marie James*
65	halfway to heaven † *Freydís Moon*
67	Fade to Black † *Morgan Dante*
74	Misery in Company † *Morgan Dante*
86	Enfleshed † *Cas Trudeau*
90	Swarm Behavior † *Aurélio Loren*
105	Recovered Contents From an Angel's Stomach † *Rae Novotny*
114	An angel song from the ether † *Rafael Nicolás*
120	Hashem Yireh † *Dorian Yosef Weber*
127	Pieces † *Emily Hoffman*
138	Paradises † *Rafael Nicolás*
146	Contributors

THE ANGELS AT HARVEST CHURCH

Freydís Moon

Content Warnings: explicit sexual content, mention of snakes/snake bites, off-page transphobia

ON A SWELTERING SUNDAY MORNING, an angel hollers verses from behind a sturdy pulpit your father built in 1993. His name sneaks between twelve-packs at the local mini-mart, whispered like gossip in a town surrounded by swampland and built on the back of too many miracles. Dusty vans are parked along the dirt road outside Harvest Church and travelers wander inside to listen, sitting shy and quiet while you tap your foot in the middle pew. Sometimes you want to tell them to go back to where they came from. Big city reporters with gold strung 'round their necks, helpless coupon-cutting townsfolk from the neighboring county, missionaries burrowing beneath borders to catch a glimpse of gilded wings.

But who are you to tell them to leave? You're the one who stayed, after all.

Your mother used to call him *holy man* and your father called him *blessed*. Now your mother has lost her voice, your father won't look you in the eye, and they're both muttering amen with the rest of the congregation. The angel has a face made for magazines, sharply cut and old in the eyes, as if centuries have been neatly tucked under his ochre skin. You remember finding him beautiful and wondering what that made you, to want a holy man, to look upon the pastor and silently pray for forgiveness. Years have come and gone since then, but sometimes you still catch yourself praying.

"See, the Lord is here," the angel says, gripping a well-worn bible in one hand and the pulpit in the other. He shifts his gaze to where you're curled against the pew and does not look away. "For he serves those who serve him. Our shield, our provider."

The owner of the local gas station pulls nails from a wooden box. Rattles pierce the air like a baby toy, like a warning, and the angel plucks a cottonmouth from the squirming mass inside. The bite-shaped scar on your thigh stings at the sight. You remember his fingertips on your leg, and the snake coiled around his wrist, and fangs deep in your skin. He'd cut your hair that day, snipped your ponytail with a pair of sheep-shears, and while the venom worked through your veins you heard him say, "Be glad, son of Adam, for you were unmade in the beginning and now you are perfect."

Son. Adam. What strange, wonderful things to call you.

You watch an immigrant from Mexico City limp down the aisle with one foot turned backward and a loosened kneecap, catch a glimpse of rosary beads rolling across the milky skin of a woman with a swollen belly, and hear tongues go wild with rapture. Snakes flash their teeth, people seize in the presence of glory, and the angel does not look away from you. People have left all they've known to find him, yet he has sought you.

You, the farmer's child, exalted and exiled, a simple beekeeper, wanted by God's most revered, most feared. The thought permeates in your groin.

The crippled immigrant rejoices on steady legs, barking "Gloria al Padre, y al Hijo, y al Espiritu Santo. Estoy curado!" You listen, and you nod, and you say *hallelujah* under your breath, wishing you could speak the language you'd been forced to forget when your grandparents traveled west, west, west. When your family pushed roots beneath a dilapidated town. When you were born in a leftover place where an ageless angel healed the sick and turned daughters into sons.

The faithful disperse, crowding in the dirt lot with their casseroles and chicken gizzards, assembling meals on paper plates in truck-beds. The skeptics chatter, meandering around Harvest Church like vultures surveying a sun-ripened carcass. You know the moment you are alone with him, seconds after your parents take their leave. Your mother slides a paper fan into her purse, your father eases the double-doors shut, and you feel their grief like an eternal bruise. The angel studies you. His eyes are molten and alive, his body a compilation of contradictions.

"Come here, Cristiano," he says, and you go to him.

He takes your chin between his fingers and heat rushes upward, downward, everywhere. This is not the first time he's touched you, but it's the first time you have the courage to touch him without being told. You run your hands beneath his buttoned shirt and find the gnarled scars above his shoulder blades. What was it like to lose them? you wonder. *What do feathers smell like when they burn?*

"You belong to the King on Earth, do you not?" he asks. He follows your jawline, still in the midst of remaking, and drops his palms to your waist, still curved and supple. You nod, of course you nod, because yes, of course yes.

"I do," you say, and open your mouth. His knuckles slide over your tongue, probe your willing throat, wet your swollen lips. Faith is sacrificial, but church is worship.

Every Sunday you arrive, sit patiently, and await your time with the angel, with God's first creation, the favorite, the fallen, who forged your inhospitable body into a livable vessel. The congregation pretends not to listen, but they hear just as well, and the miracle-chasers pretend not to be jealous, but they envy you. You, who was once draped from throat to ankle and veiled like a bride. You, who is called seduced and seductive, sacrifice and punishment. You, who has adopted a roughened voice, wide shoulders, untamed desire. You, Cristiano Castañeda, who belongs to him and you and *he*.

The angel kisses power into you. He tastes like ash and pomegranate, like smoke and apple tart, and you wish to know what flavor he finds in you.

"Honey," he says, so suddenly you shiver. "You taste like pollen and nectar and Eden."

He peels your shirt away, removes the binder constricting your ribcage, and when he hoists you onto the window nook, you see the Virgin Mary reflected in his galaxy eyes. Sunlight pours through the stained glass at your back, etched into the image of the Mother, the Child, the Wise. You are a kaleidoscope in his arms, in this church, and you can't help the sound bubbling behind your teeth.

"I belong to you," you say, the same way you would a nightly prayer.

He puts his mouth to your copper skin. Tugs the only dress-pants you own down your thighs and over your ankles. Birdsong flutters outside, as does hushed conversation and cautious prayer, but you are enraptured. Taken. Completely and utterly his. He buries his fingers inside you, crooks his knuckles and strokes your front wall. Hot breath coasts across your trembling mouth, and he says, "Look at how you've grown." His thumb works at you—your clit, your cock, your becoming—the place where your body has entered its own version of manhood.

Being with him is like speaking in tongues. You are out of control, flooded with holy, holy, holy, eager for anything, everything he has to offer. You brace on the windowsill, pitch your hips into his hand and wait for permission to come. Each movement matches yours. When your waist jumps, he pushes deeper, and when you ease onto the sill, he massages your slick cunt. It's when you're gasping and shaking that he pauses, reaching inside you to stroke and knead and rub.

"Not yet," he says.

You make a wounded sound, one he's familiar with, and you do what all worshippers must, as all devotees do—lift your knees, spread your thighs, become an altar. He has only undressed once, the first time he took you, and you will never forget how his skin felt against yours. But today, like most days, he unbuckles his belt, opens his pants, and fills you. You cling to him. Clutch his fine-boned face and rake your fingers through his golden hair. Take comfort in his grip on the underside of your thigh and lean into his hand on your tailbone, holding you upright, keeping you close.

This is for him. You are for him.

"Child of God, who freed you?" he asks. His cock is heavy inside you, stretching you wide, stirring heat in your belly.

"You," you say on a hitched breath. Sometimes you anticipate a forked tongue to flick between his lips, but it never does. He kisses the boyish sounds from your mouth, fucks you hard and quick, until you're babbling pleadingly, cooing and shaking, flushed entirely and begging to come.

Finally, the angel says, "God's image failed you, but I have made you mine, made you perfect, made you glorious. It's true, is it not?" He thrusts into you and you feel the button on his pants push against your pelvis, his smooth skin meet your pulsing dick, his cock twitch and throb in your depths.

"It's true," you whimper, grinding shamelessly against him. "I am made to be yours, my King on Earth, my Morning Star. Have mercy, please."

Again, he kisses you, and moves his hand to your cock, working you to bliss.

You clench around him, gush and flutter and squeeze him with your body, moaning pitifully against his lips. He empties himself into you on a handsome sigh—comes in thick, hot ropes and takes your jaw in his hand, fingers set hard against your cheeks. You look at him and see fire in his eyes. Brimstone. Chaos. Rebirth.

"Come to me tonight," he says, breathlessly.

You blink through a haze of pleasure and nod. He has never asked you before, but you would never say no.

He is your maker, after all.

He kisses you one last time before dusting his hands down your body. The reverence in his stare is enough to make your knees wobble. Faith keeps you steady, though, filled with burning heat and heavenly purpose. He helps you dress, as he always does, and whispers gospel in your ear as you walk to the door.

Before you leave, he puts his lips to your throat. "You are holy, Cristiano," he says. "Holy and mine."

"Yes," you say, and turn to kiss the Devil on the mouth. "I am yours."

I KNOW MY FATHER

Dorian Yosef Weber

Jacob sends his progeny across a stream.
He is alone
and then there is the flesh of a man beneath his hands.
smooth, supple arms try to push him to the ground and
Jacob, grabbing the terrifyingly beautiful stranger,
plants his feet and pushes back.
they are sweating and grunting,
the sound drowned out by the babbling of running water.
when our father doesn't let himself fall back onto the dirt,
there is a gentle touch on his hip,
fingertips skimming flesh
pale and stretched tight as a drum skin,
and, beneath the tickle of callouses,
the violent wrench of bone out of socket.
Jacob cries out, but he does not let go of the man
whose touch has broken his body.
the sages say our father knew an angel,
but here in the light of the dawn, there is only a man.
Bless me, Jacob demands,
unyielding.
Bless me.
Bless me.

Bless me the way you bless your Father.
the man softly touches his lips to Jacob's,
as they writhe against the iron bonds
of each other's grips.
the man's mouth dribbles lower, and lower
still. *Your name is now Israel,* he breathes
against sweat-slick skin,
for you have conquered both man
and divine.
Israel throws back his head,
the violent, powerful ecstasy of holiness
shaping what will touch the lips of generations.
They will not eat of the hip
and future children will look to their father
as they grapple and change and ache, as
they tear apart their bodies
in self-shattering bliss.

SEASONS OF GOD

Angela Sun

<u>Content Warnings:</u> suicide, graphic violence, body horror, undertones of sexual harassment and grooming, mentions of rape, misogyny

FRANCIS WAS FIFTEEN when Rui was born on the other side of the world, pushed out between bedsore ridden thighs and blood-soaked rags, held by midwives who knew a doomed labour when they saw one. By then, he held the poise of a religious man, and wasted long, sun-drenched days shadowing the monks, who consumed their mornings with farming and afternoons transcribing the scriptures. His family had hoped to instill some acumen and piety in their eldest and heir, sending him off too young. Neither Francis nor Rui knew their mother.

The juncture in Francis's life arrived some ten years later. The plague wandered its way into their town and made a martyr of Father Guillaume, who Francis secretly wished was his father. Grief struck him like lightning, jaundiced him; hollowed him out like a river through the bedrock. There was no return to nobility after that, only the clergy: the fixture of his idyllic childhood.

He was on the cusp of thirty-three when he arrived in the Far East, legs jellied from the endless journeys at sea. Alongside him was Father Phillip, a man who preferred the language of the locals and reduced himself to wordlessness around Francis. The men, brown-skinned and quick-witted, pointed somewhere inland at the great expanse of pale earth locked between grey skies. The priests rode on black donkeys and carried their bibles in cloth bags that slung over both sides of the saddles, gently thumping against the donkeys' backs with every step. Some weeks later they arrived at a village. News travelled fast: the village chief, having gotten the letter days ahead of time, saw them and bellowed out a welcoming. He shook their hands, shifting his eyes between them like a nesting bird.

The villagers gathered in the square. Most oversaw their presence with casual curiosity, the arrival only a facsimile of what they had heard all over the trade routes, what seemed almost overdue. By mere afternoon, the news relayed its way to the bedridden uncles and small children.

By night, it reached Rui, who had avoided the crowd in favour of sitting in the field all day. She had been half-contemplating killing herself. Two meters of rope tucked in the mice-chipped corner of their barnyard, no date in mind – a tangible promise, nonetheless. If not dead, her father would sell her soon. Her age planted the mark, and the winter made sure of it when the frost choked out half their crops overnight and stunted the rest. In the yellow light of dinners, the lamp emanating so weakly with only a lick of oil left in the font, she could see her daddy growing tired, had thought he only needed to tolerate her until the men or the fever took her. She already held the reputation of a spinster, but was a woman nonetheless, and could fetch a price higher than the neighbor's stud pig. The thought closed around her neck like a fist, and uprooted her from the smoke of the village, far into the blusterous open air of the fields.

In the field, the sweet earth smell eased her throat open; let her breathe again. Dusk was carving across the sky, sifting through streaks of white cloud. She turned and headed home, slipped past Auntie Huang who clicked her tongue then gestured to the newcomers. The two small figures were right across the river, still talking to the chief. In the reddening light of sunset, they looked like canine teeth jutting out of the ground, a mouth closing around the whole bloodied sky.

—

The first real business for the priests to undertake turned out to be grisly. An early morning in late spring, Liu Ping unlocked their barn door to the sight of her son's feet swaying above their bed of straw. She collapsed on the ground and howled until her husband came, who held her and shuddered, wretching himself into a belly ache. Francis pushed his way through the simmering crowd and gripped their hands.

"You will see him again," he began. "We'll pray for him. We'll pray for your family, too."

The husband looked up; his eyes soldered shut with tears. Francis's pale, foreign face pressed close enough to anger him. "You're not needed here," he said.

Francis nodded. "You can always come to me," he whispered. "I'll be there."

A day later, after the weeping, the mother came and knocked on the priests' door. "I want you to explain what you meant by what you said."

He opened his leather-bound bible and read a passage to her, then another. By the time they finished talking, the sun was dipping past the burnt bronze sky, a gentle chill weaving its way across the room.

She wanted to believe it. The force of wanting intoxicated her, had her light-headed the whole walk home. By the end of the week the couple convinced each other of a Christian burial. Both priests read at the service: Phillip in Mandarin, Francis in their native French. The parents, transfixed, left footprints so deep that the dusty soil pressed into something clay-like, yellow tiles split at the edges. Both would be baptized by in a month's time.

In Rui's dreams, she'd see the son's sweet breathless face, a ripple of bruises hooked around his neck like a collar. Then he'd pull her under. *My wife*, he'd say, *you've come for me*. She opened her mouth and swallowed earth, the soil and maggots, her father working the shovel. The boy smiled up at her, teeth bloody. *I love you*, he said. *I love you; I love you—*

Rui blinked awake. Her limbs were calescent and leaden, the sweat on her back flashing cold as she rolled under the open air. Her father would not marry her to a dead man, she thought. Too little money, too little pride. She thought of the wildflowers nestling at the edge of their crops, the white bursts of stardust, and the leathery leaves with veins running deep from the stem. The image put air into her lungs, and she drifted into sleep again, easier this time.

It was an uncharacteristically hot day, body heat clinging to her like gauze. At dinner her father leaned in close and peered into her face. "Did you know the Lius converted? I wonder if they still want a bride. The poor son," he shook his head, "he would have wanted to be married."

"He killed himself," Rui said.

"Don't you think his parents would have wanted to see him married?"

"Maybe."

In the night, sleepless, she watched the moths quiver around the dying oil lamp. Outside the crickets were sizzling, and the sound sliced through the heat wave. A stray dog barked at a phantom prey, and a voice broke the skin of earth like sapling: *I love you; I love you...*

Rui snuck out, half-drunken on shame, half-sobered by fear. She skidded down treacherous footpaths, skinny mud lines that twisted and dropped down in fits and starts, through the thorny tall grasses, not caring where she was going until she saw the gap in the trees ahead of her, the emptiness dipping down into the cemetery. Right in front was the boy's grave, the mound of earth still freshly dark brown.

It occurred to her then that her father could still kill her. Bitterness washed up her chest and cut at the base of her throat. She wanted to see if the boy was buried in wedding clothes. The sight swam up to her face, the two of them laid side by side. She clawed at the soil, starlight spilling into her mess. The grave yawned open, inchmeal, into a chasm. Then slowly she hit softness, the pink of flesh where a coffin should be: something feathered. She could not stop. She pried away clots of soil from the grave. A grotesque knot of torso, gleaming with streaks of blood and iridescence, a fractured tangle of feathers, and pallid bones that ran thick and tumorous into its spine. The face was lodged beneath the earth still, but the soil shifted and moved over the planes of its jaw: *my wife—*

Rui woke up to dawn. Her forehead was wet. A bat was softly jostling its body into her window, the paper outlining its silhouette. She wanted to spit something out, held her hand up to her mouth, and saw black soil lining the beds of her fingernails.

—

Spring rolled into summer, brought forth dandelions and pear blossoms in full bloom, turned the riverbanks pink with blankets of newly dead flowers. The priests had dedicated themselves to the building of the new chapel and school. Every day, men paraded into the village, carrying carts of brick and mortar on mule-back. They kicked the dirt up into the air; the chapel perpetually suspended in yellow ash, mottling the once-white glare of daylight. Father Francis spent his afternoons preaching in the square. Some days, at dinner time, they'd knock on his door and ask for a piece of his mind on a philosophical dispute. Some days, he was led around by a worried local to see the mother's persistent cough or the uncle's diabetic foot, asked to pray on it for a little good luck. By then the plague had slid off the sad shrine of his soul like debris, and sickness had returned to its primordial beauty, encased in oil and writing. He enjoyed his work immensely, thought it was proof of his own righteousness.

Increasingly, the villagers came to his door to confess their sins. Many stayed outside, unwilling to show their faces. Some came in, kneeling at his feet, asking for his forgiveness. There was petty theft, and gossip, and beatings, and rape. Men and women who scoffed at religion during the day came to him like scorned children and heaved up decade-long secrets. Always he promised them of the mercy of God. They brought food in return; thought he was a godly conduit like the Emperor or Bodhisattva. Their old gods sat polished and portly inside temples, with fruits left to rot in the lingering smoke of incense. They were no strangers to worship; Francis began to realise.

Rui tapped on his door late one night. By then, the summer light stretched out forever like a strange, ossified purgatory. She hid at the side of the building with her back to the wall. Francis opened the door, saw nothing but the barren footpath and the lake-grey sky.

"Hello?" he asked.

"My father is trying to marry me off," she said.

Francis paused at the voice beyond the door before speaking again, staring straight ahead. "Do you want to be married?"

"No," Rui said. "But I can't fight it."

He pondered this for a second. "I want to see you," he said.

Slowly she twisted her body and came around to the front door. A young girl with a round face and short figure, hair coiled into a knot. The priest lodged his body in between the doorway. Recognition was crawling up his nerves.

"How old are you?" he asked.

"Eighteen," Rui said, feeling that her age was a grievous matter.

"What's your name?"

"Zhang Rui."

"Rui," Francis said. "Your father has told me already."

She frowned. "What?"

"I cannot divulge what was shared with me in confession." He ruminated over the conversation. Prices and self-pity and jealousy — of not having a coveted daughter, of having all his sons die on him; his woman, too. Life laid bare to him as a desolate, losing war. He wanted God in his graces.

"What does he plan to do?"

He thought about how to answer her. "Have you ever been outside of this part of the country?"

"He means to sell me faraway?"

"I cannot answer that—"

"You have to help me," she interrupted, red in the face. "You're meant to stop this."

"I'll think about it," he said.

Francis chewed on the inside of his lip. He did not know what to do. Rui nodded, turned around, and left. At night she dreamt of the boy again, grabbing her under, no feathers anywhere. She was certain she had conjured the scene from her own imagination.

—

Francis stood outside Rui's house for an hour before seeing her and her father, their slight figures heaving baskets of wild chives on their heads, the flaxen cords fraying at the edges. *Will you eat with us? Would you come inside?* The priest needed to talk to Rui alone. Old Zhang closed his mouth and felt disrespected, looked on at their distancing figures with skepticism.

"When I was a child," Francis began, "I was raised by the clergy. I was surrounded by men and women who had devoted themselves to God, sworn never to be married. I swore the same vow myself."

Rui tilted her head up at him. The afternoon sun pierced through the atmosphere like a knife; she had to squint at his head, half-shrouded by light. "Can I do the same?"

"We can arrange that, I think," Francis said.

—

She moved into the priests' residence soon enough, facing little hassle except for her father grabbing Francis by his arm and whispering *you're an arrogant bastard* into his ear the day she finally left. The priests called out her name one morning at mass; said that she felt a calling to God and was graciously supported by a magnanimous, poor, widowed father. Eyes swarmed the Zhang household, held him hostage: he could not leave a conversation without praising his devout Rui once or twice. Francis recalled Old Zhang's tallowed sight, milky with gauze. *He'd want revenge*, he thought, and knew it to be the truth.

He was teaching Rui to read. Like most peasants, she was illiterate in even her own language. But Francis did not deem Mandarin important, and thought he did her a favour by choosing Latin, its balletic vowels and gossamer-like consonants. He made her memorise the first line of the Nicene Creed. Rui repeated the sounds so often that it sounded more ambiance than language, like the whipping of river reeds under the wind.

At mass, he made her stand up and recite the line to the rest of the attendees.

"It is God who made this possible," he told them. "It is God working through this girl."

The children, sitting cross-legged on the ground, gawked at Rui, astonished. She sat down and felt the gaze of the villagers burning into her back.

She was getting used to it. Every morning they sat down and he read the bible to her, fiddling with the recurring words. *Deum. Lumen. Verum.* She was a slow learner, perplexed at the endeavor of pronouncing anything polysyllabic.

"De-um," Francis said. "Not Day-on, not Day-m."

"Deum," Rui said.

"Watch how my mouth moves," he said. "My lips close at the last consonant."

She mirrored him as he mouthed the word.

He shook his head. "Open your mouth wider at the first syllable. Hold it."

She stretched her mouth around the "De—" like a listless smile.

The priest reached out and pushed her jaw down, his thumb on her bottom teeth, grazing her lip. His hand was so cold that the fingers on her chin almost stung, tender like scabbed new skin hours after he moved away.

"This is how open the word should sound," he said. "You understand?"

Rui shut her mouth and closed her teeth together, then nodded.

Francis got up and moved to his chest of drawers, got out and unfurled the letters they had gotten from other missionaries. He pushed them across Rui's desk. They were curled at the edges, moth-bitten and yellowed. On the page, sinuous, undulating lines looped across in black ink.

"I wanted to show you," Francis said, "how these letters were written in French, Spanish, English and Portuguese."

She peeked at a page beneath the writing, a drawing slipping out in sight. "What's this?"

Francis pulled it out. An inked portrait of Mary and the angel Gabriel, him pleading to her, wings stretched skyward.

Rui's face went pale. She recognized those wings, those wide patches of feather, thickly layered like a raven's. Only she had seen them white and greasy with bone marrow, laid in a boy's shallow grave.

"Who are they?" she asked.

"That is Mary, the mother of Jesus, at the moment she was asked to conceive the child of God," he answered. "The creature asking her is an angel, whose name is Gabriel."

"What's an angel?"

"A messenger of God," he said. "It's beautiful, is it not? The sacrifice she made?"

She could not answer. She stared into the soft curves of Mary's cheeks, her dark eyes upturned to the face of the angel. The black ink of the angel's wings had bled into the coarse paper, ran thin like the bristles on an evergreen pine. Then she felt sickened, and moved away.

The weeks fused into each other like viscera, business hemorrhaging into daybreak. Francis lost track of mornings talking with Rui and afternoons overseeing the chapel, dust collecting on the barren floorboards.

He had not lived with women before. In his youth he grew up under the shimmer of Mother Mary, outlined with gold and crushed purple, the oils and egg yolks congealing under the hard air. Coarse brushstrokes weathered into cliffs and canyons, the paint rising where her robe meets her face, where her halo splits from the desolate ruins behind her figure. In church he saw the sisters at choir, harmonies lapping over each other like a retreating tide. He knew their innocent faces, milky-white, freckled like eggshells. In town, then at the ports, he saw women, in cotton bodices crosshatched with flowers and heavy gowns falling around their feet. They looked out of the balconies of brothels and the windows of horse-drawn carriages, their eyes grazing past Francis's robes and cloak. Heat flushed down to the base of his neck. The understanding came to him: he could not be absolved from temptation. He peered into their faces and grasped at the meekness and the God-fearer in them. Faith was an olive branch. In faith, he was clean.

But Rui knew nothing of sin, anyway. She came to him as a helpless maiden and grew to him like a disciple. He fell asleep to the procession of missionary work and woke to the impasse of her beliefs, her irreverence at all things sacred and her humility at work. He began to like the sounds of his words in her mouth. Rui talked like all the peasants, fast and harsh, hardened the words up like chewed meat. He wrote to his brothers in the clergy and described how the scriptures sounded then, like a folk song passed through hard-laboured men.

—

At the bottom of the creek, the ceaseless current flowing into the river, a slate of rock jutted out like an overbite. Autumn leaves floated across the stream, orange-tongued and brown on the underside, hearth fires speckled with rust. But the days still held the last flashes of summer, baking the water into fog on sweltering days where the rock itself shimmered with heat. In the crisscross slashes of sunlight and water, Rui glimpsed the angel again. The refractions of his hunched body, caught between the humid air and the crest of the waterfall as it hit the ground. The twisted cords of his wings were water-logged and bloating, curled forward. From here she could smell the fester of skin and muscle saturating with parasites. Then, before she could step into the water, he was gone.

She dreamed of the boy again, of outstretched hands, white and swollen with water. A trail of algae cloistered around his mouth. He could not speak, only open his lips and let blood trickle out, drooling past his chin, snaking down his neck.

She flinched and writhed in her sleep. The brunt of it propelled the unevenly legged bed into the wall; woke Francis on the other side. Soon enough, he was knocking at her door. She opened her eyes to a room clogged with darkness. There was no window, only the sliver of moonlight filtering through the old bark of the roof beam, its fibres thinning down to translucency.

"Is everything alright?"

"Yeah," she said.

Francis leaned his head on the other side of the door. He woke up choked by a fever, the words scraping past his swollen throat. "I'm finding it hard to sleep."

"I'm sorry."

"It's the weather," he said. "I'm afraid of the incoming winter. Even now I lie awake and shiver when a gust of wind blows across the room. My hometown was never this cold."

But it was so hot that Rui was clammy everywhere her skin folded onto itself. She was sobering from her dream. There was no angel. Only this village, only this house, only this man.

Francis was shivering on the other side. He closed his eyes.

"Can you hear me?" he asked.

"Yeah," Rui said.

He wasn't really thinking. Rui had been in his dreams. She laid underneath him like a rug; the rest was hazy. He wiped the sweat from his brows and smeared it on his shirt.

"Can I come in?" he asked.

"No," Rui said. She rolled out of bed and backed away from it. Her heartbeat pounded in her chest.

But Francis wanted to see her. There was something fantastical about it, dreaming of real people: he owned a piece of her that even Rui herself had no idea of. He wanted to see the vision of Rui and the real girl eclipse each other, coalesce into something new. He missed her, felt feverish and close to God, like the prophets in delirium. The night air closed in around them, squeezed in tight.

He could hear her breathing on the other side. He rested his head against the door, closed his eyes, and nodded off into the morning.

On the other side, Rui sat in the furthest corner. Nothing but a ring of dust swirled around the ray of starlight leaking through her roof beam. The rest dissipated into darkness. She closed her eyes and thought of the angel. *Whatever you ask of me*, she asked, *make it quick*.

The village was noisily asleep. On the edge of the land, field mice rustled through the tall grass. The boy's grave was green with seedlings, worms ravishing what lingered on his bones. They spat out the offal, punctuating the soil with traces of hair, cartilage, and feather. No one would notice anything wrong, except for the child who ran face first into the ground, tasting soil, grass, and something like the smoke of incense.

—

When the first snow hit the ground cold enough to hold its shape, the village was almost entirely Catholic. Every Sunday, people congregated around the new chapel, sat quietly in the coal-warmed halls and heard the priests' sermons echo around the arched ceiling. Outside the wind rattled on; shook the skinny and naked tree beams out, startling the shield bugs nesting on the swell of branches. Winter snaked down quietly and grew mean; killed everything but the weeds. No family was exempt from the scarcity of last year's stockpile; the villagers lost half of it to the weather and half of it to the landlords. But religion was sweet on their tongues if not their stomachs: made them happy to sing, happy to worship a god whose own son was starved thin like the rest of them. Christianity came to China and slotted in just fine, helped grease the soreness out of poverty. They were going to heaven. It did not matter.

That winter, old man Zhang, who skipped service every week, nursed an ulcer in his stomach until it bled through something in him. He laid on the ground until he thought he saw a man standing above him, bleeding through his stomach with towering alabaster wings folded behind his shoulder blades. Old Zhang picked up the axe beside his dwindling timber and headed to church. Religion did not sweeten him, it robbed him of a good bride price, of a daughter who ate at his table every day and could not deliver his reward. He walked with only a shirt on his back and summer slacks, thin and frost-brittled by the gnaw of the wind, sky already dark despite the time. He walked across the frozen river, the ice six-inches thick, his feet beating out the pulse like a drum. He strolled into service, halfway through the reading of the gospels, and stepped up to Father Phillip at the top of the podium. Then he threw the axe into his torso.

Screams erupted from the crowd. The villagers scrambled to cover the children's eyes, smuggling them out of the room. Auntie Huang flung herself at Old Zhang, who shrugged her off and continued his hacking. Rashes of blood sprayed across his face and torso, dripped down his shirt and the sinewy muscles of his arms. Dimly he recalled the days in the field, the reaping of wheats. Phillip's stomach grew blurry. He was red everywhere, his skin, his organs, the cotton of his robes.

Francis and Rui were at the back of the room. The sight of her father shot panic up Rui's spine with a spasm. She stood up. Then Francis grabbed her wrist. "He'll come for us next," he said, voice vitreous from a cough. "Stay hidden."

"Don't touch me," she said.

His fingers dropped into the icy air. "He came because of you," he said.

He brought her into his home. He brought her – defenselessly, magnanimously – into his home. He was confused and ashamed. Then he grabbed her face, squeezing at the base of her jaw. "This is because of you," he said, voice low. The winter cold had long choked out his composure. Beneath him, Rui grappled with his hand, feet kicking the ground.

Old Zhang made his way to them, his body slick with blood. Rui caught him out of the corner of her eye and barked out something unintelligible. Francis turned around, and Old Zhang pointed the axe at them.

"Are you fucking her?" he asked.

Francis paused in shock. Then he shook his head, looking between Rui and her father.

Old Zhang shook the axe between them. He raised his chin. "You don't get to fuck her for free," he said. "Give me my money."

Francis, incredulous, started to laugh. He laughed so hard that he dropped Rui, who raised her hands to her bruised jaw. Red marks gilded the contour of her face, and already the purple was blooming to the surface of her skin. She looked around. The church was almost empty, all the villagers gone except for her father and the priest.

"I'm not giving you anything," Francis said.

Old Zhang raised his arms and swung, the axe slipping from his hands, grazing the skin of Francis's shoulder and tumbling off the stage. Then he threw himself into the priest, knocking him into the ground. They wrestled. Blood-soaked, the acid of Phillip's stomach lining clinging to Old Zhang's skin, they pressed teeth and nails into each other, bruised cheeks and cracked the cartilage of their noses again and again. The room dwindled to the wet sounds of their movements, like they were the pumping heart of the church.

Old Zhang looked up and saw Francis's blood-streaked face. Francis looked down and saw his swollen eyes. Old Zhang looked up and saw his cankerous mouth, his white, lustrous wings. He swung a punch into the face before his nerves pulled his muscles back into recognition, and he kicked himself backward. Francis could not look; he could not look at all: his eyes burning already. He moaned into his hands.

The creature crawled toward Old Zhang. He was naked and luminescent, his flesh covered with scales and feathers and mucus, strings of sap coating his skin like a newborn. His wings unfurled, then, almost stretching the entire length of the stage, beautiful, opalescent. Old Zhang watched him, enraptured, growing delirious.

The angel turned to Rui. She looked back, unsteady.

"What now?" she asked.

He opened his mouth to silence. Grey light filtered through the smog of the winter sky, illuminating the blood tracing the seams in the floorboards. He shook his head. Then he pointed to her father on the floor, slack-jawed and beguiled.

She nodded. The angel leaned forward, enveloping Old Zhang with his own torso. Then he leaned down, spine bent, and tore his hand into Old Zhang's ribs. The crunch of cartilage and bones; then he held his heart in his hand, red dripping down his arm, thick as honey. Rui thought of roses, wild ones that grew on the outskirts of her old house. She thought of the bees that nestled between the petals, their wings crystalline under the sun. They did not worship the nectar; they were themselves divine.

Francis was still moaning into his hands, blood trickling down the crevices between each finger. His eyes were hemorrhaging, as if fissuring from his skull. He could hear Rui, her footsteps encircling the chapel, making her way to him.

"I love you," he said.

"*Paenitet*," she replied. "I don't."

Then she brought the axe down over his head and made a clean ending of things.

—

Winter pulled the village into a long slumber. Snow stretched out into the fields as far as the eye could see, then softened into rain. When darkness finally retreated from the mornings and surrendered them to spring, sprouts erupting from ice-cracked soil, the long night hours of whispers had become obsolete. Starvation had driven old Zhang into the church, then into the icy river. The tragedy wore off its spell, looked less like a myth and more like banality. Rui sat on top of the chapel roof, overlooking the early blossoms and the awakening butterflies. The hills beneath tumbled into the horizon.

She smelled soy sauce and garlic and the sizzle of cooking oil rising through the chimneys, then heard the clatter of metal and porcelain interlacing through the conversations. There would be dumplings for the New Year, then firecrackers in the village square. Then later, after the grandparents are drunk and the kids are asleep, after the bellies are filled, there would be singing.

RESTA CON ME

Ian Haramaki

Content Warnings: graphic descriptions of dead bodies, mentions of alcoholic/abusive parent, violence, open door smut

ELIA STARED DOWN AT THE BODY that had been dumped in the nave. The woman's wide, glazed eyes weren't quite as unsettling as the grin on her face, stretched further than possible. Her hands clawed at her face, fingers rigor-locked into strained curls. Equally curved was her spine, likely shattered into pieces from how it contorted.

"Poor creature," said Nicola, the bishop training Elia. The bishop seemed bored, scrubbing at the dappled stubble on his chin and humming in thought.

"Another possession, Your Excellency?" Elia asked. He swallowed hard, barely managing to not vomit.

Nicola nodded, folding his hands behind his back. "No doubt, Father Elia. That's the fourth in this past week?"

"I think so. I... I wish they'd stop leaving them in the middle of the church." Elia dabbed at his forehead with the cuff of his sleeve.

Nicola scoffed, beckoning Elia to follow him to the library. "Somebody else will deal with her. Let us consult the literature and see if we can't solve this matter."

"Of course, Your Excellency. Do you suppose it's a specific spirit? A demon? Who?"

Nicola flashed him a smile, gaze lingering. "We shall find out."

The two passed through the cloisters, spring blooms beginning to open to the warmer temperatures. Dozens of flowers bordered the lush green grass, hedges trimmed into shape. When he had time to himself, Elia loved sitting on the benches in quiet contemplation, watching the bees pollinate the garden. He breathed a sigh of relief, grateful for the peaceful imagery before they crossed the threshold to the library.

While the gardens had the gentle buzz of life, the library was almost silent. Soft footsteps on stone tiles and the occasional, gentle sound of papers shuffling was the only thing to be heard.

Nicola beckoned Elia closer, leading him to a set of shelves toward the back. His hands shook from the thrill; books were a rare commodity before he joined the church, and while he had more access here, he hungered for whatever knowledge he could get. The books were chained to the shelves; they were particularly rare texts that couldn't be removed without penalty. Elia had never been allowed access, but Nicola's authority would clear them.

"Try not to be *too* excited, Father Elia," Nicola whispered, followed by a chuckle. His hand trailed down Elia's back, stopping at the dip of his waist. Elia's face burned, pale eyes meeting the charcoal black of the bishop. His skin prickled under the bishop's touch, lips parting slightly.

"Do you two mind? This is a library."

A gravelly, irritated voice came from the main aisle. Elia didn't recognize the clergyman glaring at the both of them. His hair was long and dark, shining like the fine eastern silk he'd seen merchants carrying. His skin was a warm brown and absolutely dusted with freckles. His eyes were similarly dark to the bishop's, but there was a warmth behind them that Nicola lacked. Elia leaned away from the bishop's grasp, drawn to this mystery man.

"Apologies," Elia spluttered. "The bishop was just trying to calm me down, we'll be out of your way shortly, Father–?"

"Daniele," the man replied, "But you may call me Dani."

Nicola scoffed behind him. Elia could *feel* how the bishop rolled his eyes. Nicola replied gruffly, "And what are you doing in here, Daniele? You are not one of the attendants."

The way Dani's hands tensed around the book in his hands was difficult to miss, knuckles going white. Elia made mental note to never refer to him as anything but Dani.

"Well, Your Excellency," venom dripping off each word, "I've just transferred in from Venezia, and I am in charge of the tomes here starting today. Now, if you would mind yourself, and your hands, it would be appreciated."

Nicola's hand trailed along the small of Elia's back before pulling away. Elia's face was on fire. He was so ghostly pale it would be obvious, his ears scorching hot in further embarrassment.

"Father Dani, we're researching the string of demonic possessions that has been happening recently. Do you know anything of it? We were attempting to look back here for research materials."

"I was informed, yes. You won't find anything here, follow me to the archives."

Nicola jeered, "I've known this library longer than you, Father Daniele, I shall stay right here."

Dani paused, face blank as he turned to the bishop. Elia glanced between them, both men still as stone. Elia broke the silence with, "Your Excellency, let me see what Father Dani has for us. It can't hurt to look everywhere, yes?"

Nicola turned his attention back to the forbidden shelves. "So be it."

Elia followed Dani quietly. They wove through the shelves, stopping at a locked door made of a dark stone. It was intricately carved with dozens of angelic visages, the figure of *San Michele* in the center. Dani rolled his eyes, shaking his head as he pulled out a ring of iron keys.

"Not a fan of Michele, Father Dani?"

"Absolutely *not*."

Elia couldn't help a laugh, cheeks warming. "Michele is one of the Lord's greatest warriors, he struck down Satan. What's not to like?"

Dani flipped through the keys muttering under his breath, "Pompous, thick-headed..."

The mysterious priest shook his head, finally picking out the correct key for the door. The sound of the pins turning echoed through the library, earning a hissed "Quiet!" from another of the librarians. Dani cast him a glare before pressing the door open.

"You speak as if you know Michele personally, Father Dani." Perhaps Elia should be upset with such insinuations about *San Michele*, but Dani was too funny about it.

The archives were smaller than he'd imagined. Elia knew the archives existed, but he'd always imagined they were a vast network under the library, as far as the eye could see. Still, a room half the size of the main library was nothing to sneeze at. Elia scanned the room in wonder, shelves full of chained books and artifacts locked behind glass and metal.

"You've seemed particularly excitable about the tomes, Father Elia..."

"I-I didn't get much chance to read at home. I've learned so much since joining the church, and I just love learning everything I can. Is that silly?"

"Not at all. Just don't get so excited you let bishops get handsy, hm?"

Elia spluttered, face going hot again. It wasn't his fault! And who was to say it was any of Dani's business to begin with? Ridiculous man. Nicola was important to him. That was all.

Dani appeared bemused, pulling out a book of matches to light the candelabras. Elia huffed and took a few to do the same. The room slowly came into a faint orange glow, vision returning to them. Dani then reached for a high shelf to pull a black leather tome. Next to it was a small, delicately painted icon of the Virgin, gilded in gold and glowing even in the dim light. Elia made the sign of the cross, folded his hands together, and bowed before acknowledging Dani again.

"This is the best text on demons in the entire world. If it can't tell us who we're working with, I don't know what will. Too many Princes and Dukes of Hell to count, I swear." Dani scowled as he examined the book on a nearby lectern, gently pulling the cover back. Elia signed again as Dani thumbed through the pages, illustrations of horrific beasts in black india ink on vellum. Demons with multiple heads, many with twisted bodies of differing parts stitched together.

Dani smiled. "They're not going to jump off the page, *mio caro*."

Elia blinked, shaken out of his fear by the endearment. He leaned forward to look at Dani's face. Dani's eyes flicked to meet his. "Is this the same priest who was scolding me for letting the bishop get close?"

Dani rolled his eyes. "Perhaps. I don't trust him."

"You've only just arrived, how could you say that? He's the *bishop*, Father Dani."

"Forgive me, Father Elia, but you're rather naive. I'll simply suggest you be careful around him. He has power over you... I would hate for something bad to happen because of it."

Elia straightened up again, brows furrowed. What a presumptuous, frustrating man. And so casual with him! Unbelievable.

"Here," Dani said suddenly, pointing to a particular page in the book. The illustration showed a nude angel's form with an owl's head riding upon a black wolf. It wielded a great blade and its large, animal eyes seemed to stare at him through the page. "Grand Marquis of Hell, Andras. *Testa di cazzo.*"

Elia gasped, covering his mouth with a hand briefly before smacking Dani's shoulder. "Profanity inside the archives, Father!"

"Now I know you're not upset about me referring to a *demon* this way." Dani shook his head, turning the book so Elia could look closer. "Look. He's known for sowing discord and even killing his summoners outright. It would explain why he's wreaking havoc in the city. He's very subtle in his possessions, which is likely why he hasn't been found. But we can keep an eye on the signs, explore the city. I'm sure he'd love the chance to get at two priests."

"Now who's *we* here? I was going to look into this with His Excellency–"

Dani took a hold of Elia's chin, stopping him in his tracks. Elia's eyes were large and owlish, not far off from one demonic Marquis.

"Father Elia. Please, let me help you."

Elia could hear the rush of his blood in his ears, heart pounding so hard he was sure it would break his ribs. He'd spent long hours with the bishop, admiring how handsome he was even with his age, utterly smitten with how kind Nicola was to him. They had exchanged long glances and brief touches. The moment in the restricted section earlier was the most that had occurred between them. Certainly love for others wasn't strictly forbidden, but between two men? Two clergymen? He wouldn't dare speak of it aloud.

But here was Father Dani, on his first day, being so much more bold, more *direct*. Here Elia was, already taken in by this new, strange man. It should terrify him how open Dani was, but the stirring in Elia's chest said something else entirely.

"I... We can explain to His Excellency together, then. Yes."

Dani had a warm gleam to his eyes, playful smirk spreading across his lips. Elia licked his own anxiously, swallowing hard enough it was audible.

Finally, Father Dani released his chin, fingers trailing along Elia's jaw. It finally registered how warm Dani's touch was, all the more obvious when the tips of his fingers dipped just below Elia's collar. Elia thought he might faint if this continued.

Storming footsteps across the stone had Dani tearing his hand away, Elia gasping reflexively. He clutched the front of his vestments, willing his heart to calm itself.

"Does it truly take so much time to find the name of one spirit?"

Elia and Dani both glanced at the doorway, Nicola casting them glares. His gaze was particularly dark when it met Dani's. Elia could swear there was a fire burning in Dani's eyes, a brief flash of gold before it faded. Perhaps it was just a trick of the candlelight, flickering all around them. Elia rubbed his eyes, just to be sure, but Father Dani appeared the same.

"Apologies, Your Excellency." Dani's voice was cool and even. The resentment he bore was clear even behind the formalities. "Though I wonder why you didn't attempt to seek out the name of this demon sooner if it was going to take so little time?"

Elia's eyes went wide as dinner plates, fear plastered across his face. He glanced between Dani and the bishop, both staring each other down. He'd seen dogs in the streets who would look at each other this way before attempting to rip the other's throat out.

"It was unclear if it was a demon before, Father Daniele. I'm sure you understand, it takes time to diagnose these types of possessions, especially from a high-level demon."

Dani's eyes narrowed briefly. "I'm sure. Well, Father Elia and I will be going out into the city to investigate."

Nicola waved his hand several times, as if shooing a fly. "Nonsense! Elia and I were meant to investigate together. Isn't that right?"

The two men looked at him. Now it seemed Elia was a piece of meat that the two dogs were fighting over. He hated this.

"Ah, well, won't you have to remain here in case there's any more bodies found? You're the authority for the day, after all. It would be a terrible thing if the lay people felt lost. Or worse, if one of the cardinals found out." Elia chewed his lip, feebly attempting to look innocent. "I'm sure we can find time to discuss our findings later, Your Excellency."

Nicola's face went flat. His cold eyes flicked up and down Elia's body, settling on his face. "I see. So be it then, Father Elia."

The bishop left in as much a hurry as he arrived. Elia's stomach twisted; he'd never seen Nicola look at him with so much disdain. He leaned on the lectern for support briefly before Dani linked their arms together. When Elia looked up their faces were close, close enough he could feel Dani's breath across his cheeks, felt the heat radiating off of Dani's skin and through his vestments. How was this man so *warm*?

"Never mind him. Let's find this Andras together, Elia."

Dani brushed some of Elia's dark curls away from his eyes, genial smile on his face. Elia was light-headed from Dani's radiance.

"Y-Yes..." Elia righted himself again, smoothing out his vestments and stepping out of the archives. He brought his voice to a low whisper as they reentered the library. "These bodies have all come from the same neighborhood. Do you suppose we should start looking around there?"

"Yes, that seems wise, *mio caro*. Lead the way."

They made good time heading into the lower district. The river glittered with the afternoon sun, fishing boats of various sizes slowly gliding across the water. Elia sighed, wishing he could have enjoyed the day rather than search for bloodthirsty spirits with owl heads. They wove through the alleys as they came to the most poverty-stricken part of the city. Many of the people were familiar with Elia now, being one of the few clergy who was willing to aid the poor of the area. It disappointed him how his brothers would rather service the rich, going against every word of the Lord; such was life.

"I don't quite understand why a demon would attack here," Dani whispered. "Wouldn't it be more likely some rich sorcerer would send one after his equally rich enemies?"

Elia pursed his lip in thought. It was strange. "No, you're right... I've heard of possessions and attacks in the bigger cities, but usually they're on politicians and wealthy merchants. Sometimes higher ranking clergy like the cardinals... Never the poor. Odd."

Familiar faces stopped to greet Elia and introduce themselves to Dani. They took their time questioning everybody they could, perturbed to find no rhyme or reason to the possessions. There was no pattern to follow to help them predict who would be next, no area to keep watch for outside of the whole district. Elia pinched the bridge of his nose as they came into another narrow alley. He paused to lean back on the wall, gently slamming a fist against the stucco.

"Damn this Andras. I don't know what to do except wander for all the night."

A searing hand lifted Elia's chin. The fading afternoon light cast Dani in a blazing glow. The gold cross around his neck flashed even in the shade of the alley. Here in the dark, far from prying eyes, Elia felt calm. He met Dani's eyes, peered into the deep brown depths, rich like the coffee drink from the Mid East. Warm and inviting all the same, like all of Dani was.

"Don't fret, *mio caro*. I'm sure we'll find a lead soon."

The tips of Dani's fingers still burned into Elia's skin, still touching him. Elia lifted a shaking hand, slowly clasping around Dani's.

"I'm sure we'll manage together, Dani..."

The air was sucked out of his lungs, Elia had no idea what came over him. Despite the danger lurking, Elia just wanted to be close to Dani. His presence was magnetic, drawing him in. He strained his eyes to count all the freckles across Dani's beautiful terracotta-colored skin. They were like the heavens above, endless and mesmerizing.

Equally Elia was being scrutinized, dark eyes roaming all over, following every line of his curly hair, along his jaw, settling on his mouth. His heart skipped when he realized.

Dani's lips were warm like the rest of him, rougher than Elia had expected, but a pleasure all the same. The kiss was soft, tender, but it wasn't chaste; Dani leaned into him, bodies pressed together. Elia shivered at the contrast of temperatures; warm body at his front, cold wall behind him. He needed more of Dani's warmth, wanted to be wrapped up in it forever. It wasn't a painful heat, more like a fair spring day.

They held each other as Dani kissed him again, hand slowly moving up Elia's back to grip at his hair. His heart beat faster and faster, the tips of his fingers prickled as his body warmed. A soft gasp of breath puffed out from between Elia's lips as Dani's tongue glided across the lower one. Dani took the opportunity, licking into Elia's mouth. The kisses grew in fervor, desperation. Elia was in the clouds, desperately gulping down air between beats. Elia let Dani overtake him; he wanted to be consumed.

His wrists were pinned to the wall, Dani asserting himself; Elia was happy to submit. He tilted his head back when finally Dani pried their mouths apart, laving his tongue just under Elia's jawline. He moved to pin both of Elia's wrists with one hand, using the other to pull down the collar of Elia's vestments. Dani sucked hard on the skin, nipping at it over and over. Elia winced from the pain, hissing between his teeth, but he dared not tell Dani to stop.

Elia's cock throbbed, tenting his clothes. Dani's thigh pressed between his legs, rubbing against his aching member. The bulge against his hip made him dizzy; Elia had only himself for reference, but Dani was much larger. He made feeble attempts to push down the desire to see it, to touch it. His mouth went dry picturing it, and just in time as Dani was kissing him again. Elia's lips were puffing up from how hard they kissed, from how long it had been. His arms were beginning to go numb from being pinned up and he wanted more of Dani. He *needed* more. Perhaps they could give up for the day, go back to the rectory to find a corner. It was sin, what he wanted Dani to do to him, but it would be blissful all the same.

A woman's scream broke their focus. Elia shoved Dani back and his eyes went wide, both looking in the direction of the sound. Elia recognized it.

He took off running, dashing through the street, not a care for if Dani followed him. The house was tucked back into a corner, faint candlelight coming out of the dusty window. Elia came up to the door and pounded on it with a fist. "Mama? I heard you scream, please come out!"

The silence had ice forming in his veins. His mother would always answer the door, if only so she had a chance to scream and call him terrible things. She was sometimes slow in her wine-drunk stupors, but never failed to answer.

Elia lifted his fist but couldn't find the will to slam it against the wood, letting it fall to his side. He could hear Dani calling out for him back on the street, but he couldn't dare face the other priest like this.

His hand hesitated above the knob, a brief moment to wonder if it would be this easy. The metal was cold to the touch, but the heavy wooden door swung open without a fight. Elia was quiet as he stepped inside. The front room had a rotted sofa stained with wine, a cold, ash-filled fireplace, and a small kitchen in the back corner. The candlelight he'd spotted came from said kitchen, a single one set on a chipped wooden table. The only other light came from the moon through the back window, full and nearly at its zenith.

Elia peered into the dark to his right, searching for the bedroom door. It was open just a fraction, but pitch black inside. His heart thumped in his chest, the rushing sound of his blood flooding his ears, a high-pitched whine ringing that made his head ache. She couldn't be dead. His mother couldn't be dead.

As terrible and unforgivable as she was, he didn't want her to be dead.

Elia creeped up to the door, cringing as a board creaked underfoot. He'd heard quieter groans from the ships in the harbor!

He jumped out of his skin as the door swung open. He blinked, realizing that the figure that had stormed through was the bishop. Elia heaved a sigh in relief, leaning forward to clutch his shaking knees. He made the sign of the cross before righting himself, meeting Nicola's gaze. His eyes were glassy and black, staring him down.

"Your Excellency, thank goodness it's just you. Is my mother here? I swear I heard her scream. Were you tending to her?"

"Worry not, Elia. She has been taken care of."

His shoulders relaxed further, flashing the bishop a warm smile. "Thank you, Your Excellency. But... why are you here?"

Elia stared back into the bishop's eyes, round and glistening. There was a nagging at the back of his mind, something that he couldn't place.

"I was in the area, searching for this Andras of course. I heard your mother scream, and so I came to her aid. I didn't realize she was your mother."

Nicola took a step forward; unconsciously, Elia took one back.

"I see... Y-Your Excellency... I don't recall naming the demon we were searching for."

The whites of Nicola's eyes were shrinking, filling in with black like ink in water, sockets larger than any mortal man's. Elia swallowed audibly.

"And I don't recall you being an adulterous whore, Elia." In a blink the bishop was gripping the collar of his vestments, tight enough his air was nearly constricted. "I can smell him on you. I can smell your *arousal*."

The bishop pressed his nose to Elia's neck, sniffing loud in his ear. The bishop moaned, hand trailing down Elia's chest. Elia's body shook violently, wracked by fear. He lifted an unsteady hand, holding up his thumb and first two fingers. "C-*Crux sacra sit-*"

Nicola's hand wrapped around Elia's throat, squeezing tight. Nicola lifted him off his feet, and Elia clawed at his hand, feet kicking at the air. The bishop's grip went tighter. Elia gasped fruitlessly, eyes rolling back without air. His body went limp, and darkness greeted him.

—

Elia was freezing. His limbs were numb, muscles stinging with pinpricks as he tried to move his hands. His neck was stiff and, contrasting the rest of him, absolutely on fire. He lifted his head, eyes struggling to open. The first thing he noticed was that he had been stripped bare, skin exposed to the chilly underground air. He was surprised to find he recognized where he was, dozens of carved stone tombs lined the high walls, cobwebs shrouding the faces of the dead. The catacombs, then.

Elia was chained to the wall, hanging off the ground with his arms stretched apart. In the center of the room lay a sarcophagus carved from marble, one of much more importance. It was flat, but had intricate engravings. He stared down into the face of *San Michele*, recalling Dani's bitter reaction towards him.

San Michele was certainly not in this place.

Elia thanked the Lord that there was no sign of the bishop, nor was there any sign of an owl-headed demon. He cursed Nicola under his breath. Damn him. Damn him! Did he truly betray his vows to the Lord all because Elia dared glance at another? He stared up at the chiseled ceiling and begged God, hoped beyond hope that He would send Dani, or that Dani might find help. Anything.

While he didn't fear his afterlife, he was certainly not yet ready to die, nor was he interested in dying by whatever torture Nicola and Andras had in store for him. He felt that was reasonable.

"I suppose you should be thanking the good Lord that you're awake at all."

Elia rolled his head over to Nicola, standing at the base of the steps into the catacombs. He could barely croak out the question, "Why?"

Nicola's eyes were still large and black, circular orbs that glistened in the low candlelight. "Why do this to you? Because you are a traitorous whore, as I said. Running off with that young halfwit who's only just arrived. It is I who has taught you everything you know, who has courted you. How easily you are swayed!"

Elia swallowed, throat burning as he tried to speak again. "You were my teacher, Your Excellency. You are a bishop. Why a demon?"

Nicola stepped up close to him, knife in his hand. It looked old, rusted, and dull; a cruel instrument meant for pain more than precision. He pressed the tip to Elia's belly, just above his navel. "The poorest of this city turn away from God the most. They needed to be taught a lesson, to fear the Lord again. Never do I see their faces for mass, not even holidays! Andras is simply a tool. I will bring him into this world to dole out his punishment, and then I will remove him in time."

"And my mother?" Elia stared down into Nicola's owl eyes, finding only coals of demonic rage. Whatever humanity Nicola had had disappeared the moment he let Andras infect him.

"She was a drunk and profligate who was a scourge on all she encountered! That she was related to you only made it sweeter. But don't act as though you miss her; I've been there for all your crying, Elia."

Rushed steps echoed from the opening into the chamber, drawing the bishop's attention away. Nicola's grip relaxed a fraction, knife point dropping from Elia's stomach. Elia thought he might burst into tears when Dani rushed into the room, nearly crashing into the wall.

"Get away from him!"

Dani's eyes glowed gold; there was no mistaking it this time. The dim light of the candelabras around the room couldn't compare.

The knife was pressed back into his stomach, hard enough to draw blood, but not enough to pierce into his gut. Elia grimaced, teeth grit as the wound flamed in pain. Dani froze, staring down Nicola with all the rage of heaven in his eyes.

"If you approach me further, this whore dies. Understand?"

Dani lifted both hands to keep the peace. "Nicola. Andras doesn't control you. We can remove him together."

Nicola scoffed. "I let him in, *rovinafamiglie*! You can't stop this. I will offer this simpering excuse for a priest to Andras, and then the people of this city will remember to fear God."

Dani snarled, smashing a fist against the wall. The stone cracked under the force, stunning Nicola into silence.

"*What are you, priest?*" Nicola spoke, but it was not only his voice. Something darker, raspier, unused to speaking in human tongue. "*You are no man.*"

Dani shouted, "Elia, close your eyes!"

Elia didn't hesitate, a flash of white light blazing that penetrated even through his lids. He hissed through his teeth, turning his head away from the glare. His wrists burned, aching as he was yanked off the wall. He heard the crumbling of the stones, felt heated hands on his skin, cool metal like plate armor on his body. There was a beating of wings, a soft touch like feathers that brushed his shoulders.

Dani whispered to him as he set Elia on the floor, "Open."

Elia blinked, gazing up at Dani. Was it him? He was similar, but so much was different. The black hair that flowed like midnight water was scarlet like the first light of dawn, his freckles glittered like the sparks of a fire, his eyes pupilless golden wells of light. Dani's armor gleamed, golden plates carved with intricate filigree.

"Daniele..."

Dani scowled and clucked his tongue. "I told you not to call me that. Anyway, be not afraid or whatever. I'm going to go kill that fucking demon now. Would you mind exorcizing him for me?"

"My voice–"

Two fingers brushed along his neck, warmth coating his raw throat like honey. Dani helped Elia to his feet, both glimpsing Nicola clutching his eyes and screaming. Smoke rose from under the bishop's hands, the scent of burning flesh filling the chamber. Dani dropped a gold cross into Elia's palm and sunk down into a sprinter's start.

"Elia, now!"

Dani moved with unnatural speed, wings flapping just once to launch himself at Nicola. His sword flashed into existence in his hand, swinging it at the bishop. Elia held up the cross, pouring all his focus into Nicola. Now his voice came in clear.

"*Crux sacra sit mihi lux, non nunquam draco sit mihi dux.*"

The bishop grabbed hold of the sword, black blood spurting across the wall. Andras' strength kept it in place, but Dani's overcame, blade cutting through the bishop's palm.

"*Vade retro satana, nunquam suade mihi vana.*"

Nicola's scream was like the screech of an owl. Elia's heart pounded in fear. Andras raged at the angel in front of him, long black claws of his uninjured hand raking across the armor.

"*Sunt mala quae libas, ipse venena bibas!*"

Dani pulled his blade back, swinging across Nicola's midsection. The two halves went flying apart, a shadow bursting from inside the bishop and filling the room, snuffing out all light. More unearthly screams filled the catacombs, so loud the Earth shook around them. Elia dropped the cross, pressing his hands over his ears and collapsing to his knees. A chill wind raked across his body, and the last he heard before the cold overtook him again was Dani shouting his name.

—

This time, Elia was warm. It had been years since he'd been to the ocean, but he recognized the gentle lapping of the waves. A breeze blew over him, tousling his curls over his face. He wrinkled his nose and peeled his eyes open, sitting up with a groan. He didn't know where exactly he was, but knew this was a very grand coastal villa. It was made of light colored stone, red carpets and curtains on every surface. He threw the covers off the bed, the linens soft and cool, and stepped onto the floor. His clothes were loose and white, but they were not his vestments. Those seemed to be lost forever.

Elia found Dani on the terrace. He was leaning against the parapet, golden wings folded behind his back and glittering in the midday sun. Elia couldn't help but reach out to touch them, earning a quiet giggle from the angel. An entire angel of God before him, though one of the Watchers... He wasn't sure what to make of it.

Dani turned to him, his clothes equally breezy as Elia's. Not the gleaming armor he'd seen in the catacombs. He still looked so much like a man, but he supposed humans were made in the image of both angels and the Lord. The breeze threw Dani's scarlet strands of hair this way and that, gorgeous no matter where they landed on his face.

"I've watched you a long time, Elia. I have seen your heart, how you carry yourself, how you act on what you believe. I have grown to love that about you..." Dani's bronze, gold-freckled hand reached out to touch Elia's cheek. It was warm like the sun; Elia wanted Dani's hands all over him. "I... have grown to love you,

Elia. And I wonder if you could do the same in return."

Elia couldn't help a bashful smile, glancing down. "I think so, Dani. How could I deny my angelic savior, and one so handsome?" He looked up again, eyes lidded. "I would like to continue what we started in the alleyway. Would you mind?"

Dani needed no further instruction, hauling Elia into a searing kiss. Their lips crashed together, arms tangled up in the other. Elia had one hand carding through Dani's silken hair, the other grabbing at the base of a wing for support. Dani moaned in his ear from the touch, shudder wracking his body. He hauled Elia back to the bed, tossing him down on the sheets. Immediately there were teeth and tongue on his pale throat, licking and biting at the skin to bring red marks to the surface. Elia let his head fall, spine arching as Dani ground their hips together.

"You're so easy to mark as mine... *Mio caro–*"

Dani's mouth began to trail lower and Elia moaned louder. They stripped each other of their clothes with swift hands, bare bodies colliding together. Dani was lithe but well built, broad shoulders to support his great wings, equally broad chest his pale hands could roam across. Elia glanced down to admire the rest of Dani's body, sucking in a breath as he glimpsed his cock. Of course the Lord would bless his angels handsomely. He'd felt it in the alley, he'd had faith, but sometimes seeing was believing.

Dani chuckled, reaching over for a jug of olive oil to slick up his fingers. He reached down to press two against Elia's hole, prompting Elia to spread his thighs. His head fell back, breaths coming in rapid as he adjusted. Dani worked him quickly and he adjusted just as fast. He watched Dani stroke himself to coat the length of his cock in oil, mouth watering in his want. The head pressed to his entrance, and with just a few shallow thrusts, Dani was inside of him.

Elia gasped, reaching up to claw at his own curls. He was full up, Dani's throbbing heat pressed against a spot inside of him that sent sparks through his veins. Every snap of Dani's hips sent more pleasure through his body, had his head in a cloud of fog. Every movement forced another whiny, breathy sound out of his lungs. His own cock leaked and twitched, threatening to spill over at any moment.

Dani kissed him hard, tasting every corner of Elia's mouth, and Elia was happy to let him. This was all he'd ever wanted; all he could ever want again. Was it sin, to be with an angel this way? He hoped the Lord could forgive him for this, and for every other moment they sinned together in the future. He couldn't make an accurate prediction, but certainly it would be hundreds.

Teeth sunk hard into his neck, and Elia shouted as he came suddenly. His eyes shot open, shudder running up his burning spine, muscles tensing around Dani. Dani groaned, pounding into him once, twice more before liquid heat filled Elia.

Dani collapsed onto the bed next to him, the two gazing at each other. Dani leaned over to kiss him once more, and Elia smiled.

"I doubt I'll have a problem learning to love this, my dear angel, Dani."

"You won't regret it, *mio caro*."

SERAPHIM
Ian Haramaki

IAN HARAMAKI 43

WITH WINGS LIKE MADELEINES

Dorian Yosef Weber

<u>Content Warnings:</u> references to eating disorders, sexual assault/abuse

DURING KEDUSHAH, you're supposed to stand with your feet together. A scholar once said that the angels stand on a single, rigid leg, and we hop up on toes pressed tightly together to imitate them. I have knock knees. I can't stand like that. My legs hurt at the end of the day.

On Yom Kippur, we fast to be like the angels who do not need to eat or drink. If I don't eat or drink, I may never be able to start again. It wouldn't be the first time. I don't consume anything during the day while I'm around my community. I'm allowed to feed myself for the sake of my health, but I can't help but feel shame that they are able to be like white-clad angels while I can't. I guzzle water straight from the tap and choke down crackers at home in the dark of the night. I can't turn the lights on because of the holiness of the day, but I wouldn't even if I could.

In Sodom, the men of the town attempted to lay bitter hands on angels disguised as men. Fire and sulfur were sent down to raze their city. The image was so holy that Lot's wife turned to salt, an offering to the angels whose warning she ignored, when instinct drew her eyes to destruction the way a tongue is drawn to the gum where a tooth used to be. There was no fire and sulfur for me. Maybe there would have been if I was able to be more like an angel.

In the smoke-filled hall of the L-rd, an angel pressed a hot coal to a prophet's lips to purify his mouth, made filthy by the despair of watching the splendor of the angels' worship. I often lay my own hands on my lips, rubbing and pressing and laying my thumb down the middle like the angels did when they silenced the Torah knowledge that I have been scrambling to regain for my entire life before I was born. I either got this habit from the spectrum I'm on or, if you ask Freud, a result of neglect that has driven me to masturbate with the wrong pair of lips. I don't feel purified by my fingertips on my mouth, though. I am no angel. My fingers are not the blunt tip of a coal taken from an altar by a pair of tongs. It is said that G-d made the first pair of tongs on the eve of the first Sabbath. It is unthinkable that a lowly human would burn their hands beside a fire in pursuit of the divinity of creation.

I have a friend who is an angel, but only sometimes. He believes that the antichrist has come at other times. He says that we are in the final days. I say yes we are, and how wonderful it is, until he goes to sleep and wakes back up and forgets. I am no angel. I am not bringing about the end times with trumpets and a body made of fire. I'm a man who sleeps alone, a member of a tribe who is waiting for a messiah. No one voices the fear that he may never come. That would be heresy, but there is only so far a person can run from doubt. Time is running out, son of David.

The angels climb up and down a ladder that our father Jacob was blessed enough to see. I have to climb a ladder in the storage room at work every so often. I don't like it. I don't trust the metal not to snap under me. I don't like flying on planes, either. Maybe I would trust the wings if they were my own. It's probably a good thing that I will never see the ladder leading into the sky. It would probably make me sick. I could see demons, though, if I wanted. I would just have to rub the ashes of a cat's placenta into my eyes.

Our demons are not evil. They are mischievous and wicked, but so is one of the four beloved Seder children. The king of the demons flies up to heaven to learn Torah with the angels. I wonder if he feels like as much of an intruder as I do in the temple. A gnarled creature in the middle of a perfect crowd. *To my right Michael and to my left Gabriel, in front of me Uriel and behind me Raphael, and over my head G-d's Shechinah.* And in the middle of it all, me, dirty and human with slick thighs and a wicked tongue, so unlike an angel.

AND THE MOUNTAINS MELT LIKE WAX

Tyler Battaglia

<u>Content Warnings</u>: fire, death, panic attacks, body horror

SOME PEOPLE WERE BORN with the mark of the Devil. At least, Abel's mother always said as much. She would not profess to know what this looked like, just like she wouldn't profess to know anything else about God's love or the Devil's machinations. But she said she knew it most of her life: that many people were unlucky enough to be touched not by God or an angel, but by the Devil.

Her children—Abel and his two sisters—would often argue when they were young about which one of them was touched by God, which one by the Devil, and which one was simply boring. Since there were three of them, a holy trinity in their mother's eyes, it made sense that their mother would have collected one of each. As children, being the normal and boring one had seemed like the worst lot they could draw, even despite their mother's God-fearing warnings to not stray too far from the path of light on either side. The Devil and God both had punishments fit for children, after all.

Abel still thought about it all sometimes. Whether he was born lucky, unlucky, or a normal bastard like the rest of them. Lately, he thought that his mother would certainly say that his life was touched by the Devil. Lately, he thought they had been wrong as children, and that he would give anything for a life a little less touched by anything at all.

Maybe that was why Abel was recklessly climbing up a mountain in just-above-freezing temperatures, Cain following on his heels. It was foolhardy. It was absurd. It was pointless. It made Abel feel a little more alive again.

And Cain was off-duty, so he would probably have nothing to say if Abel fell and died.

Abel climbed over yet another fallen log that indicated he was off the beaten path. He was out of breath in a way he never would have been six months ago, panting at the simple physical exertion that once was commonplace, routine, *easy*, nothing at all. He asked, "If I trip and fall off the mountain, will you at least go get help?"

Cain woofed. Abel paused on top of the log, looking back at the big black lab that was dutifully following him down mountain trails, and sighed.

It wasn't fair to Cain, maybe. But not much about life was fair to anyone, was it?

Abel thought of being blasted with heat, of choking on life-ending smoke, of being so out of breath he couldn't think, and of knowing that meant worse for all the people around him. He thought of a dozen crucifixes hanging askew on the wall, shimmering in and out of existence like heat mirages, next to boarded-up windows through which no one would escape alive.

Abel closed his eyes and braced himself against the log. His mouth went dry and his throat constricted. His head spun, like he was being dragged backwards with vertigo, even as he held himself as still as humanly possible. His skin prickled with phantom sweat from an imaginary heat. He was in an impenetrable furnace. When he could no longer bear it, he scrambled for his backpack, trying to find his bottle of water, but started to sway, started to lose his balance, started to tip—

Something snagged the leg of his shorts and pulled. Abel used the momentum to resettle himself on the fallen tree. He opened his eyes and looked down at Cain, the beautiful, big, dumb dog with his teeth latched firmly into the denim of Abel's pants.

Off-duty or not, maybe Cain would not be the death of Abel after all. "Thank you, Cain." There was a pause where Cain stared up at him, wide brown doe-eyes in the face of a dog, refusing to give up on Abel. "I'm okay," he promised. "Who's a good boy?"

The dog let go and Abel slid off the log to the other side of the path. He tested his footing on ground that seemed to shift impossibly under the soles of his shoes. It was still hot. Unseasonably hot, even though the air was cold. Hot enough for Abel to think that something was wrong, as if he had inexplicably developed a fever. He'd deliberately chosen to come up to the wooded mountaintop when the risk of forest fire was next to non-existent, and it was a cool day at best, so whatever was causing the heat couldn't be *good*.

Whatever had started the fire that day in the boarded-up apartment hadn't been *good*, either.

The heat and the cold and the dizziness of it all made Abel shake for a moment, staring at a fixed point among the trees, at nothing in particular, until Cain nudged the back of his knees, urging him to keep moving. Always to keep moving.

Abel turned slightly, back toward the dog, and leaned over to pet his ears. "I'm only petting you because you're off duty," he reminded Cain. "And you're not supposed to be working. Even though clearly your work ethic is better than mine."

Abel hadn't been back to work in months. They hadn't fired him only because it would be grounds for a discrimination suit. He could tell. Because who wanted a firefighter who had panic attacks at the sight of a lit match?

At least one of the two of them was earning his keep, he supposed.

But the heat was still there. The terrible, oppressive heat. It wasn't fire—God, he hoped it wasn't fire—because there was no smoke. If where there was smoke, there was fire, then where there was no smoke, there was no fire. He couldn't accept anything less.

Abel was still afraid. He couldn't confirm it *wasn't* fire. Instinct told him to look despite his heart seizing up in his chest. Instinct told him he was supposed to do the saving. If he didn't look, he'd never know.

The words came unbidden to him, but someone else had spoken them recently. Local papers had plastered his face across various pages—the front, at first, before he was relegated to footnotes buried on pages seven through ten. His photo and the photos of the dead. The story, too. At least the official one.

Eventually, someone found it online. A stranger. She had called him.

"Don't you ever wonder," she had asked, "what's out there?"

Abel had said, "No."

"It wasn't a normal fire." As if Abel hadn't already known that. "People get hurt all the time by things like this. If you share your story—the real story—you could help people. And maybe you could find a new purpose. Don't you want that?"

Fucking *chills* had run down Abel's spine. He didn't know who the hell she was, how she knew anything about him, why she gave a damn. It was true that he had spent months aimless, wandering, afraid of too many things, barely able to breathe or get out of bed some days, even with Cain's help. He had known he'd never fight fires again and had wondered what in God's name came next. If anything came next.

Abel said "no" again and hung up on her.

She'd called back. Left a voicemail. Reminded him of her name and told him to look her up online. And he did—he found out she was some kind of hunter of the paranormal. Exposer of truths and lies alike. She seemed to have a habit of finding people like Abel, getting their stories, the real stories, out there. She found the people who had been touched by God, or an angel, or the Devil, and she put them back on their feet among the rest of the world, those fortunate enough to have been touched by nothing at all.

It all sounded like bullshit, no matter what Abel had seen in that apartment last fall. No matter what had started that fire. He'd saved her number, despite his better judgement, but he hadn't called her back. He still remembered the slogan he'd seen on her website:

If you don't look, you'll never know.

Fuck that, Abel thought. Yet, still he found himself moving slowly—slow as Hell—toward the source of unseasonable heat on the side of a mountain in March. Cain followed at his heels.

The trees were dense on this part of the mountain, so Abel didn't see much of anything until the heat started to get more intense, intense enough that he thought that he was getting close. And at first all he saw was light. Bright light. Like someone had taken the sunrise peeking over the horizon and zoomed in. Abel checked his smart watch. It was well past dawn.

For a moment, Abel thought of turning back. He almost did. But then Cain woofed softly as he moved past Abel to lead instead. Maybe he knew Abel well enough to know he was going to back down. But why would a dog care? Then again, Abel thought, maybe Cain just smelled something interesting.

"You're supposed to follow me," Abel pointed out, even as he picked up the pace to keep up with the dog. His lungs strained. A side effect of smoke damage, he knew—because the panic attacks evidently weren't enough for him. "Slow down."

Cain kept going, and Abel kept following, but it didn't take long to find trees that were somehow askew. Forced down and away from something, leaning back like they were trying to avoid touching something reviling. Or maybe the opposite—trying to avoid touching something they were unworthy to touch.

And there, there was the light and the source of heat, Abel supposed. A small crater in the middle of the woods on the side of a mountain. And in the middle of the crater, a figure.

Instinct kicked in. Someone was hurt. And even if Abel was in no shape for emergency response, being a first responder had been his whole adult life. He picked up his pace, jogged over to the crater, even as his lungs started to strain, even as something in his mind screamed and screamed—

He closed his eyes the second he laid eyes on what was in the crater.

For a moment, he couldn't describe it. His mind held two competing thoughts: that was the most beautiful thing he had ever seen and that was the most horrifying sight he had ever beheld. Something terrifying and perfect. Terrifyingly perfect. Perfectly terrifying.

He couldn't make sense of it. He couldn't think. It was indescribable. It was awful. It was beautiful. It was Godly. It was Hellish. It was the most ordinary miracle of all.

Abel wanted to open his eyes and see what it was his mind had railed against for himself. He needed to open his eyes. He was frozen to the spot.

And then he heard Cain howling.

Cain hadn't been Abel's companion for long—and he had named him in a way that told everyone just how much he resented his need—but he had become a loved one. The ironic and petty name for an overgrown puppy had turned into one of fondness. *You'll be the death of me, someday*, he told Cain. Because Abel already couldn't fathom the opposite, the idea that maybe *he* could lose *Cain*.

Abel's eyes snapped open as he leapt forward, grabbing Cain's collar and pulling him away from the crater. Cain's howling continued, but it changed shape—it wasn't pain. It was mourning.

Or perhaps it was worship.

Losing his foot as he tugged Cain away from the strange hole in the side of the mountain, Abel fell to his knees. He stayed there, knowing he, too, should worship.

His eyes landed on the thing in the crater again. This time, he saw it more clearly, his eyes open to the truth.

The thing in the crater looked like it might have been human once. Or perhaps humans might have once been the thing in the crater. Abel recognized, at least, that they were supposed to resemble each other.

Holy, holy, holy, Abel's mind rejoiced. He wasn't so sure if holy was the right word. But it *was* beautiful, despite his fear. And somehow, someway, despite everything, Abel knew that this was an angel. This was one of the angels that Abel's mother had always wished that he and his sisters had been touched by. Not a demon, not a Devil. An angel.

Abel almost wept. He didn't know how he knew that it was an angel, but something in his mind cried out to him that it was. Like calling to like. Humans calling back to the thing that provided the blueprint for all that came before and after.

Besides him, Cain continued to howl, the sound scattering birds from the trees. The birdsong faded into oblivion. Abel stayed on his knees until Cain wore himself out, the howling, too, fading away.

"Come on, boy," Abel said softly. Carefully, reverently, he lifted himself to his feet. He took cautious steps toward the thing in the crater. It was hot—almost unbearably—but he was less afraid than he was before. It still sent his heart racing, but it was also oddly comforting. *Safe.*

Coming to the edge of the crater, Abel stopped and stood as still as he could manage. He stared down into the hole. He stared at the angel. He tried to wrap his mind around it and failed.

Holy, holy, holy.

Abel wanted to determine if it was alive, but he did not know how one determined if an angel was actually alive. Did it need to breathe, like Abel struggled to do every day? After a moment, he decided yes—for what else could be sending trembling shivers up and down the angel's body, its wings, so many wings, twitching up and down as if something still animated it?

So yes. It was alive. It had to be.

Cain sniffed at the crater and Abel crouched down to be closer to the ground. How long had the angel been there? What did it need? What could Abel do? All of his rescue training could do nothing to save him now.

The angel's eyes snapped open, all of them, all at once.

Abel yelped and fell backwards. More irises than he could count, in an array of colours—red, orange, yellow, green, blue, indigo, violet—radiant in their prisms, shifting perpetually, followed the movement. Some of them rolled loosely like they could not focus, but most locked onto him.

"You're awake," Abel said softly.

One of the angel's mouths opened. Out came a song, like the birds, like the mournful, worshipping howl. Abel's ears rang. He'd experienced tinnitus for the first time when that apartment had gone up in flames. He'd experienced it a few times since. But this was like an echoing—the song repeated in his head, would possibly repeat forever, even when the angel's mouth closed again.

Holy, holy, holy.

Abel took stock of his options. The angel was burning up—he could feel it from here—so there was no need to cover it to keep it warm or protect it from shock. It was breathing. But if it had been here for a while, perhaps it was hungry, dehydrated. Abel carefully took his backpack off and grabbed a water bottle and a granola bar. He saw Cain perk up at the sight of food, wagging his tail, but Abel disappointed him by placing both on the ground just at the edge of the crater.

The angel emerged, like how Abel could imagine it emerging from the womb of God, long limbs with too many joints bending and creeping out of the hole. It crawled up into the dirt. It picked up the granola bar and placed it gingerly in its maw, consuming it whole.

Abel stared in shock. He had been the one to provide it, but it still baffled him. An angel had just devoured an almond butter granola bar. It had contained raisins. It did not feel divine.

There was a sound, then. A choking, hysterical sound. Abel didn't recognize what it was, even while distantly realizing it was coming from himself, until Cain began to nose at his hand, press into him with gentle pressure, asking for Abel to put his hand on top of his head. His head swam. Cain saw the panic attack coming, even when Abel did not see it in himself.

The angel was still watching him. Maybe it was dizzy, too. Its eyes never remained still for long, even if they remained generally in Abel's direction. It nudged the water bottle. The bottle fell over and rolled toward Abel. He stared in disbelief. Was it offering it back to him? Did it matter? He could use it.

Abel lifted his hand first to pet Cain to thank him for and accept his comfort before he reached out for the water bottle. Something was frightening about putting his hand so close to the angel, like it might swallow him in his entirety like it did the granola bar, but it simply watched him as he picked up the water bottle. His hands shook as he popped the spout and drank from it. The water was tepid, not cold, but compared to the heat the angel emanated, it was a comfort. Soothing.

It didn't stop his head from spinning, not completely, but focusing on the water for a few moments helped.

Abel took a few breaths. He tried to steady himself. Cain brushed against him. He would be okay. He would be okay. He was far away from that place. He would never have to go back. He would never even have to talk about it again. Not if he didn't want to.

Unsure what else to do, Abel held the water bottle back out to the angel, whose bony hand reached out to take it back from him, as if understanding.

Their fingers touched. Abel was shocked at how cool they felt despite the heat of fire radiating off of it. And he understood many, many things at once: the angel's name, though Abel could not fathom how to wrap his mind around the syllables of a word that was not a word; that it had fallen here, not of its own accord; that it was not male, nor female, nor neither, nor both, that it was beyond Abel's comprehension; that maybe everything would be okay; that it loved Abel simply for being here.

Tears sprung to Abel's eyes. As a boy, his mother had told him and his sisters that God loved them and that that was why He ruled with an iron fist. Abel understood well that holy love was both pure and terrible. He had been awe-struck by it. It was another thing entirely to feel it—this angel was impossible, it was real, it was everything, it was nothing. It was here. It loved Abel because he, too, was here.

"Thank you." Because what else did one say to that realization? On second thought, Abel added, "I love you, too."

The angel nodded, a gesture that seemed incomplete somehow. It still held the water bottle, even though it did nothing with it.

They stared at each other for a long time. Cain sat nearby, right by Abel's side, refusing to move. He, too, watched the angel, but now with a quiet acceptance, as if he felt what Abel felt. They both knew that the angel could be a threat, but that it did not choose to be.

Abel's head began to hurt. He closed his eyes to block out the light, the glow radiating off of the angel's body. The relief was immediate, but so was the confusion. As soon as Abel closed his eyes, he failed to remember what the angel looked like. He failed to understand. Its loss nestled into his heart immediately, terribly. Abel's throat constricted with a grief that echoed something he'd been feeling almost every day since the fire.

He opened his eyes when Cain licked at his hand. He took a trembling breath and pet the dog before returning his gaze to the angel. It hadn't moved. It still held the water. After a moment, it held it out to him again. Cain seemed to notice, and took the bottle from the angel, gripping it in his jaws, before returning it to Abel. Abel didn't know if Cain felt anything from coming so close to the angel. But maybe the dog had already understood God.

"I'll just keep this then."

The angel cocked its head and slowly came closer. It moved in a strange crawling motion, its legs bug-like as they propelled it forward. Its wings flared slightly like they would help it gain momentum.

"God," Abel started to say. He thought that maybe that would be offensive but correcting himself or apologizing seemed strange. Instead, he took a drink from the bottle as he collected his thoughts before saying, "How did you get here?"

The angel said nothing at first. Abel wondered if it could speak at all. Everything he had understood thus far had come from its song, its touch. No words. So, when the angel reached out again, he understood what it needed from him. His hand shook as he reached out to make contact.

At first, he saw and understood nothing. He felt only the strange hot-coolness of the angel's skin. Something about it exhilarated him. And then there it was:

Fire. So much fire.

Abel recoiled from the angel at the sight of it. It disappeared when he broke contact, but it had been everywhere. Fire—everywhere. Burning. Screaming. Where Abel's Hell had included smoldering plywood blocking access to first responders, and religious iconography going up in flames, the angel's fire had been different. Just as terrible, just as all-consuming, but it had no source and there were no exits because the fire stretched into infinity.

Was it an angel after all? Was this a mark of a demon? What was the difference, and did it matter?

Abel barely recognized it when he began to weep. The image was gone, but he could practically still smell the smoke, feel the heat, hear the screams. Someone was burning alive in the next room. Something had started that fire deliberately. A sacrifice to God. Purifying fire.

Holy, holy, holy.

Abel couldn't breathe. He couldn't see. Couldn't think. He could barely feel the movement of Cain as his service dog put himself between Abel and the angel. Cain leaned against him, offering weight. Comfort. Abel wrapped his arms around the dog and allowed himself to weep into Cain's fur until his throat stopped burning and his head stopped spinning.

"Fuck," Abel gasped out. Cain licked his face to calm him down. Despite the nightmarish vision, Abel couldn't bear not looking at the angel, so he made sure to look at it again. Unsure what else to say: "You, too, huh?"

The angel didn't try to touch him again, but it opened its mouth again and sang. It rang in Abel's ears again. A mournful song. An apology. The angel wasn't sorry for everything, and maybe not even for much, but it was sorry for this.

Abel thought that he would never understand. Yet he understood.

Keeping one arm around Cain and allowing himself to rest some of his weight on the dog, Abel wiped away his tears with his other hand.

For what could have been eternity, the three sat together alone on a mountain. An angel, fallen. A child of man, wounded. A beast of Eden, blameless.

Abel thought of his mother's words. A child could be blessed by God, or an angel. Tainted by a demon or the Devil. Unburdened and alone.

Abel thought, too, of that woman's words: If you don't look, you'll never know.

Slowly calming, Abel wet his lips. He looked at the angel. The strange, inhuman thing. The thing that was more human than human. Both and neither. He found himself speaking.

"We thought the call was normal. We thought—fires are surprisingly routine, most of the time, actually. But someone had boarded up all the windows. We couldn't get inside except through the front door. And of course that's dangerous as Hell. But I went. Smoke was everywhere. And it didn't take long to find the shrine."

The angel watched. It listened. It waited.

Abel couldn't explain how he knew it was listening, but it was listening.

"There were—crosses and crucifixes everywhere. It was a nightmare version of my grandmother's house, God rest her soul. And Christ, nothing we did could do anything about the fire. Like it was impossible. But I found this man. And somehow, I knew. I knew he had done something to make the fire impossible to put out. And I—"

Abel sobbed.

"Angel, please forgive me, I killed him. I killed him because I didn't know what else to do. And angel, please forgive me, but the moment he died, the fire went out, just like that. And angel, please forgive me, but I was glad."

It was the first that he had told anyone of it. It had been impossible to know, otherwise. Everyone else at the centre of the flames had died by then, the only survivors besides Abel had been in different rooms of the apartment building. Abel had barely survived himself, nearly dying from the burns. And what difference did it make if the culprit had died suffocating on smoke or because someone had cut off his air on purpose?

But Lord, how many people had died before Abel had done it? How many were sacrificed, and why?

Was it enough for whatever unholy purpose the man had intended? Abel had saved a few of them, sure, but had it been too late?

He had nightmares, sometimes, after staying up too late at night wondering how many souls it took to summon something worse than whatever that man had already been. He dreamt of nightmarish creatures breaking through the crust of the Earth and seeking out not only Abel, but all the other survivors. Things not unlike the angel, but with no love for anyone in their hearts, least of all Abel.

"Angel, forgive me."

The angel watched Abel for a moment. Cain seemed to understand something before Abel and stepped gingerly out of the way. The dog bowed down, like he might play, but more like in reverence. The angel crawled closer. It leaned into Abel. And it kissed him.

Holy, holy, holy.

It felt like magic. It felt like forgiveness. It felt like redemption.

The angel moved away. Again, Abel began to weep.

Without knowing why he was saying it, he promised the angel, "I will never forget you. I will always love you."

One last time, the angel opened its mouth and sang.

Holy, holy, holy.

Abel closed his eyes and sobbed. His only regret would be that he did not see the moment when the angel disappeared. He only knew it was gone when the birdsong finally began to return, and the side of the mountain finally began to cool. A soft, furry pressure rested against Abel as Cain came to console him, nuzzling him, offering him softness and comfort in the face of his impossible grief. Abel opened his eyes and found that not only was the light of the angel gone, but the entire mountain was in darkness. The sun was setting over the horizon, far below the mountaintop. Much time had passed.

Only Cain and Abel remained.

Abel slowly pet Cain as he tried to soothe himself, to calm down one more time. But as the last of the sobs wracking his body disappeared, he was more at peace than he had been in a long time.

Softly, he laughed. "Maybe it wasn't so foolhardy to come up the mountain after all, was it?" he asked Cain. Cain only woofed gently in response. "You will help me get back down, though, won't you? In the dark? I can't imagine the embarrassment of a search and rescue officer having to come for a first responder."

Cain licked Abel's hand and Abel slowly stood. He looked out through the trees at the last disappearing rays of light.

He pulled out his cell phone and wondered if he had service on the side of a mountain. He wondered if he should call his mother. Or perhaps someone else, someone who had offered him a new purpose. He probably wouldn't get any reception, but maybe he should check.

If you don't look, you'll never know.

THE MOUNTAINS, THE MOUNTAINS, THE MOUNTAINS

Tyler Battaglia

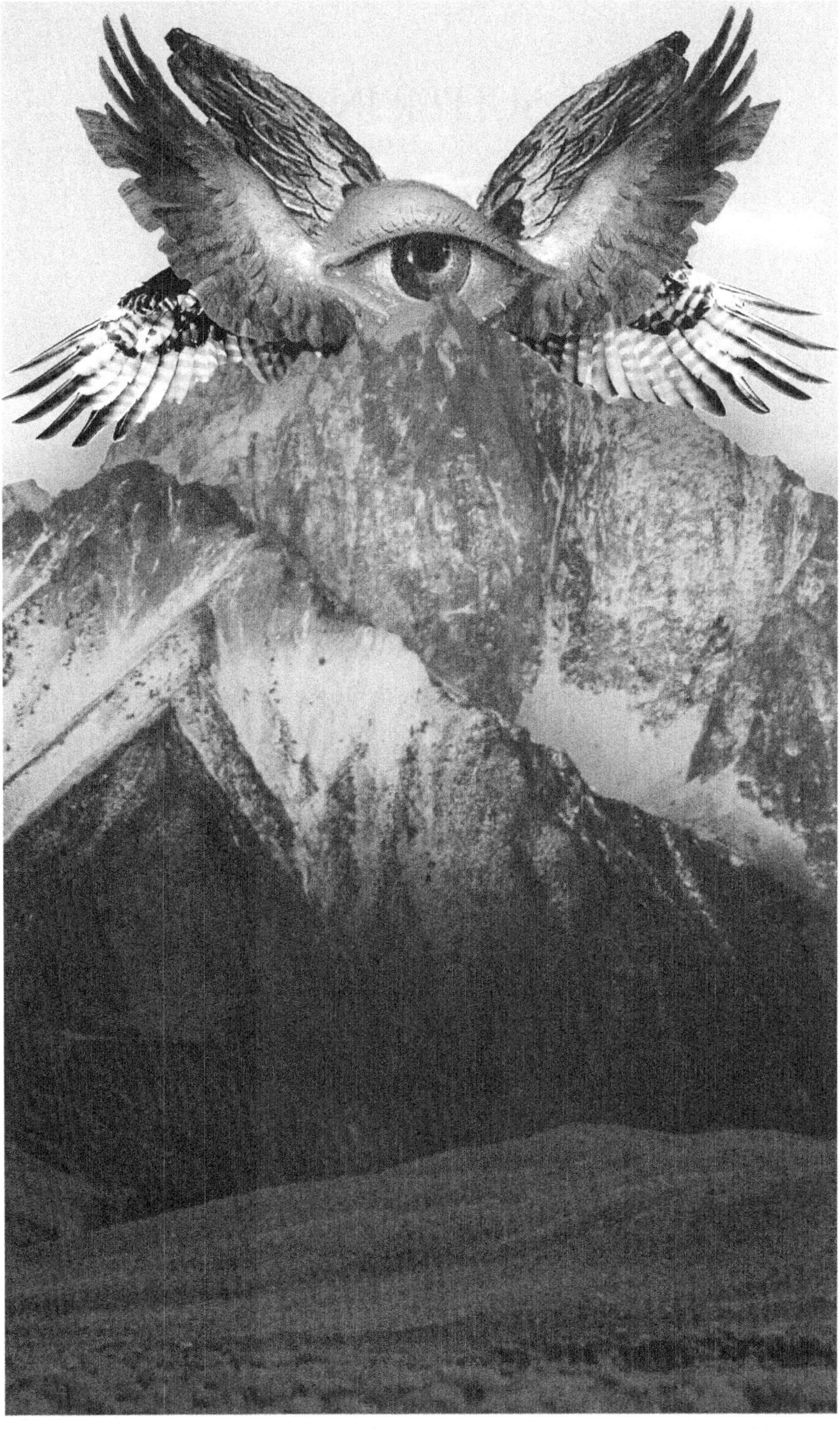

WE SUFFER IN FIRE

Tyler Battaglia

<u>Content Warnings</u>: fire, death, murder, religious fanaticism, monster/body horror

I BEGAN STARTING FIRES not because I wanted to, but because I had to.

For I am Moses, you see, and the bush is burning. The world is burning. If I start fires, I can lead the world out of its self-made Hell and into salvation. I am to be prophet. If I cleanse the world with fire, we will receive the new Commandments and I will have saved the world. And shouldn't I want to save the world? Its very soul?

The vision I have, I don't know if it is from God. The angels that I foresee crawling forth from the crust of the earth and consuming humanity, devouring it whole, bit by bit, person by person, do not look Godly. Not with their long, long limbs, their sharp, sharp teeth, their impossible eyes. But I have to believe that my vision is righteous, that whatever gave me this power to start fires, impossible fires, gave me a blessing. That the people I am burning alive are burning for cause. That with each person who dies from choking on the smoke, from the excruciating pain of immolation, I am closer to divinity for the world and for myself.

There are no other options.

I am burning the world, burning away its sins. I am burning. But from the ashes, I shall rise. From the ashes, the world shall rise. The angels will devour anyone who is not worthy, and all others shall rise. And I, I am worthy.

I decorate my sites of atonement with iconography of devotion. By calling to God, calling to Christ, I can confirm to myself that this work is holy. By burning everything down while the Trinity watches on, I am comforted that the people who die here are dying for the Holy Spirit and the grand plan of the universe.

I tell them so—that they die for the righteousness of eternal life for all that come after them. They don't fight it. I see terror in their eyes, but I know that they understand: this is the way that it must be.

With each death, I can feel something coming closer. I know it must be God, for there are no other options.

With each death, I can feel that we are closer to the precipice. We are close now, I can feel it.

I grow impatient. I know that if I can burn more, purge and purify their souls, all in one fell swoop, that I will have delivered the world to God as it was always intended to be. He will right it all. Noah guided the world through flood, and I shall do one better—I myself do the burning. I no longer wait for God's hand to guide me. I decide. I act.

I *burn.*

The apartment seems like the perfect trap. It is easy to board up the windows so that no one can escape. And I set the fire.

Perhaps it was too obvious. Perhaps God was punishing me for my arrogance, for daring to shape His plan into my own. Still, I think I have won—I am so close now, so close, and I can feel the fabric of the world about to snap into something new, something better—until the responders arrive.

Until one chokes the life out of me to stop the fire.

I wonder, which of the Commandments hold true? Thou shalt not kill?

I wonder, how many did I burn alive for God's plan? Was it ever His plan at all?

I wonder what punishment befits my sin.

I don't have time to wonder for long. Death comes with a final vision as my soul is dragged from my body. The last thing I see is an angel, sublime, crawling forth from the crust of the earth, ready to consume humanity, devour it whole, bit by bit, person by person.

Starting with me.

DIVINE BODY

Daniel Marie James

Can you taste it?
Silky liquid swirls
Over your tongue
Splattered on your cheek

Roses
Sinking into battered flesh
You call out to them
And they whisper a response
Do not be afraid
Yet you tremble
Under watchful eyes
Cosmic

Can you feel it?
Tumbling down the gashes
They take you apart
A thread pulls pieces
Back together
But wholly wrong

Masterpiece
They whisper
And you fall apart for them
Again
In an act of devotion
Is this not
Divine?

HALFWAY TO HEAVEN

Freydís Moon

I think we might be halfway to heaven, and dare I say: let's stay

Count down to midnight with me on every eve of everything we've ever decided was ours for the taking
Tuesday night diner dates / Strewn across the hood of your car—stars igniting
Breakfast in the afternoon. You, watching me, my passenger seat miracle.
How you laugh in your throat, a goddamn symphony, and I want to applaud, I want to laugh too, I want to ask:
when I laugh do you feel like there's a bird in your chest?
See, you've jacked my mouth open, shoved a dove deep, low, where my lungs flutter
cavernous and scarred and still healing.
I cough like I used to when I smoked, and feathers come up and out of me. *Do you see them?*
My love is one-sided and I'm sorry if it's heavy, but I'm tripping, babe, I'm falling. And I often wonder
if Lucifer fell too, if he crashed to Earth and dared to say: let's stay. If the angels on high
told him to chew—*the bones are hollow; they'll splinter*
told him to rise—*brother, we're only halfway there*
If he looked at<space><space><space><space>us
like I look at<space><space><space><space>you

I wonder if he named the bird
if he trailed his thumb along the tree of life, chasing God's blueprints
like I trail mine along the coffee cup you left in my Jeep, chasing<space><space><space>anything, really.

I don't know about *we*<space><space><space><space>but I am halfway to heaven
<space><space><space><space><space><space><space><space>dare I say: let's stay.

FADE TO BLACK

Morgan Dante

<u>Content Warnings</u>: mentions of heavenly violence, aka angel face-melting; mentions of nonbinary transmasc character dealing with deadnaming, transphobia, and misgendering; emetophobia

MEPH FLIPS BACK HIS SILVER HAIR and scoffs at the little field of crushed cigarette butts flowering the asphalt outside the Waffle House. "*This* is where the town's only cinema is?"

"Yep," Perse replies with a suppressed grin. There's something liminal about a Waffle House parking lot by the evening highway.

Crows bicker on the power lines above. Despite the omnipresent car exhaust, Meph's clove-like fragrance, mingling with brimstone, soothes Perse.

The demon curls his nose and looks across the parking lot at a small square brick building, with a moss- and rain-streaked sign that reads, *Blood Mountain Cinema*. Wildflowers, glistening with dew, snarl around the front—also covered with cigarette butts, stamped on and looking like little accordions, or frozen worms.

The building sits before a small hill with a rash of gold and wine-red trees; the latter color makes Perse think of Meph.

Meanwhile, Meph's harsh gray gaze slices into the little mountain town scene. Perse rubs the faded red rose on the side of their neck and thinks:

He's lucky he's pretty. And Perse sorta likes his complaining. Meph insists that he doesn't care, but if he didn't care like the "true nihilist" he was, why is he taking in so much of the area and making comments. Obviously, it must matter.

And what was Perse thinking, making a deal to brighten the most cynical being in the cosmos? *Stay with me for a year, and I'll make you happy.* Like they're the epitome of a positive attitude. Going to work, deadnamed and misgendered by a bunch of Don't Tread on Me fucks who snicker at they/them pronouns and unironically wear shirts that say, *Sarcasm is my second language*; their mom would be good friends with them.

All that, to plop globs of toxic green mix to make pistachio creme cakes for griping customers—and they're made with walnuts and almond extract! No pistachios. Supermarket bakeries are such a ripoff.

Positive attitude.

Perse digs their palm against their sore ear, as the whooshwhooshwhoooosh sharpens to a whistle. "Well, the movie starts in about five minutes, so let's go, Sunshine."

Meph waves a hand and gives a sweeping mock bow. "At your will."

Behind them, one of the smoking waiters leans over to another. "Bro, he's like, so tall."

It's true. Perse wasn't sure if people would just accept a guy with at least a dozen red tunics, silver hair, and a whole seven feet as a part of life. What they underestimated was people's need to let life go on. Oh, they'd whisper about that weirdo *way* too tall fruit who's at best from Florida and at worst a theater major at some hippie liberal arts college in Atlanta.

The tail and horns, though, Meph hides with magic; only Perse can see them, but they can just imagine their coworker Amanda going, *Oh my God, his cosplay is so good! What a realistic tail!*

As Perse's sneakers smack the pavement toward the lonely cinema, feeling themselves being watched, they fish an apple-flavored cough drop out of their sweatshirt pocket, crinkling the paper to suck it into their mouth. Even in early fall, when it's still humid, they prefer wearing sweatshirts and jackets at least twice their size to hide their boobs.

The people staring are telling themselves a story, *a story of someone they think is me, but isn't. That girl with the tattoo who likes horror movies and isn't quite right, her and her queer friend who holds the door open for them.*

As if reading their mind, Meph props open the door, painted black with a metal bar on the inside; the demon flings the entrance open and postures a polished boot to keep it in place. Even as he schools his expression, the way his tail curls like a question mark feels smug. Meph takes care not to step on any of the flowers.

Perse used to despair that no one ever got them, that they weren't perceived as who they really were. *They don't see me. They see what they want to see. Whatever fits a clear label.* But they've decided there are benefits to oneself being the only person who will ever truly know themselves. *Everyone else is missing out, not me.* And isn't it incredible that there are billions of little worlds floating around just on one planet?

Breath tasting of the cough drop, Perse sucks air through their nose. Their lungs open up as they walk on burgundy carpet, the small room with a counter and concession stand, the tight air smelling of ammonia and popcorn butter.

In the dim back of the room, there is a bathroom and two small hallways that jut out; there are only two showing rooms in total, and Perse knows that once the new superhero movie comes next week, they won't be able to see this movie with a flagging box office unless they get Meph to transport them three hours away or rent it online if it doesn't stream anywhere with a free trial. Perse only sees three people. One at the counter, another at the concession stand, and another sweeping in the hall.

Meph rubs one of his sharp canines with his pinky. "Must we stay the entire two hours and twenty minutes?"

Perse sweeps a strand of curly auburn hair out of their eyes. "Come on, I would've taken you for a cinephile." Despite the fact that they're barely even friends, they stand close to one another.

"Isn't it a horror?" Meph asks with a derisive sniff, idly stroking one of his spiraling horns. "Tsk."

They would think *oh no* if they hadn't already spent a few months with Meph. "It's more of a romance."

"Oh, you humans so love to categorize things. Romance. Horror. In Hell, it can be hard to tell bodies apart from the masses of suffering souls clamoring together. I can't separate them, much less all these particulars. When you've lived so long and seen so much of the cosmos and its possibilities, the human desire to whittle things down to as simple of labels as possible is perplexing. And really, it's a horror to believe in the farce of love."

Perse crosses their arms. "Okay, it's a horror romance. Let me guess. You don't like horror."

"I can't say I've enjoyed much new media, including films." The demon's definition of "new" extended back about five-hundred years. Which, given how long the cosmos has been around, isn't too out there.

"You don't like movies? Any movies? Dramatic? Campy? Nothing? Be honest."

"Oh, some are decent, I'm sure, but most are juvenile." Figures. If Perse presses, Meph will probably relish them with tales of seeing *The Duchess of Malfi* at the Grand Guignol and watching audience members faint. And then he'll kick his feet back on the dining table and sigh, rubbing his narrow chin and proclaiming that that was *true* art back in the day.

And yet, Perse sees themself in that cynicism, never being a fan of the action movies or Westerns their parents and grandparents enjoyed.

"Which one do you like the best?" Perse asks.

"Which film, you mean?" The demon twirls a finger around a silver strand of hair.

"Yeah."

Meph hums, and Perse admires the cut of his cheekbones as he cranes his chin. "*Phantom of the Paradise.*"

That surprises Perse, who, despite loving Seventies stuff, expected something a little more...pretentious. They nod to him. "Brian De Palma. Nice." They don't linger on the subject; Perse worries that if they tease Meph's too far that he'll duck back into his careful, polished shell.

With that, they approach the counter. Meph starts to speak, but Perse shakes their head. As much as they don't like talking to strangers, they want to try.

Perse deepens their voice, or hopes they do. After all, they can barely hear, and they've heard your voice sounds deeper to you than anyone else. "Two tickets for *Strawberries*, please."

The young woman standing behind the counter smiles, her smile kind, her skin wan except for the bluish bags under her eyes, a constellation of acne on her chin. "Sure, that'll be twenty bucks."

Once Perse and Meph are inside the bright-dark of the theater, as a bouncing candy ad plays, Perse pulls out a red bag from their pocket. "Here, split a weed gummy with me. Food and movies just feel better once the high hits. And food is like, I wish it tasted like that all the time."

Perse has only just started to like food, to stop wishing there was some injection they could take to get all their nutrients with the constant worry over looking androgynous or even masc with a fuller figure, wondering what nasty comments they'd get if they ever got approved for a mastectomy, and can they be any worse than the comments about how "she" must attract a ton of guys?

Or their mom laughing and saying Perse never needed a bib because their boobs would catch everything, or talking about how much Perse "inherited her stomach and bubble butt from her dad."

But Meph for the last few months was all about the feasts and wine. Savoring the taste of everything, and damn it, Perse realized they liked hot wings and garlic bread and pasta loaded with parmesan and oregano and tea with a slice of lime and champagne. And they were active, walking every day with Meph, and they felt good and complete.

Humans live such short and fraught lives. Why deprive yourself?

"I don't think it will be as potent for me," Meph tells them, carrying a large tub of popcorn. Nevertheless, he leans down and lets Perse without hesitation bite off half of the gummy and set the rest on his absurdly long devil-tongue. Watermelon flavor bursts in their mouth as both of them sit in the very middle of the theater.

About twenty minutes into the movie previews, Perse can feel the brain and stomach expanding, and they dig into the popcorn Meph holds. The salt stings their bottom lip where they've been chewing on it again.

When the movie starts with an establishing shot of ocean waves during a stormy day, Meph quips, "How original." Always with the cynicism before anything can really get going. Perse understands, though. It's easier to not be disappointed if you give up on committing.

Perse shushes him, wanting to actually enjoy the movie and not hear a running commentary, and already loving the hazy imagery. They'd never been to the ocean, and it always felt new and immense every time they saw it on film or in a picture. In the film, it's wreathed with mist, like the ghosts of sea monsters.

The movie, once Meph quiets his snark, is compelling, and Perse takes quiet satisfaction that even Meph can shut it for about two hours. They thought for sure the demon would at least scoff at all the romantic parts.

About halfway through the film, Perse looks over out of the corner of their eye at their demon companion.

Meph is fully leaning into the back of his seat, his back ramrod straight. He stares at the screen, not with his usual flat or sardonic expression. In fact, Perse can't say they forgot what emotion looks like on his face because they don't think they've seen anything but the brief hint of glee when he set a murder of crows on a guy who was bothering Perse.

The whoosh in their head becomes a fog spilling through their entire brain, and a piercing ring, and they see—

Crashing ocean waves.

Lightning.

A group of winged men laughing in a grove.

An angel's face melting its one-hundred eyes all over Perse's bloody palm, a grimace swirling like wax.

brother.

what have I done?

what have i done whathaveidone w h a t h a v e i d o n e

his face is melting on my hands. i can't scrub it away

it's still there, his eyes his eyes his eyes

he can't feel. he can't let doubt in. he can't feel. he's a follower of Lucifer, he's a monster, and everywhere is Hell. that's all, and he doesn't care.

nothing matters god will scrub the world clean destroy all the demons and that's it no salvation no hope no love. heinrich will watch him die in the lake of fire and no no no not even he cares enough.

[an ocean shore, an old man's dead body caressed by seafoam as rose petals fall from the bleary sky; he falls, they always fall]

he's my grace i can't get him back i'm alone again   *fade to black.*

Perse leans down with their head in their hands and starts to cry. Cry for their lost life, all the years they've dressed or acted a certain way to make everyone else but themselves happy. Swallowed their deadname like poisoned gum.

it wasn't my fault i've had to spend all these years surviving, and only surviving. but i should be free and happy. i could shave half my head again, buy a tux, burn all my old dresses and replace them with turtlenecks and button-up shirts

But the universe is so big; angels have fought wars in cosmic spheres they can't even fully visualize—just nudging the blurry image splits their migraine into a thousand new migraines.

And angels died. The universe is so big, and they've lived their life based on the opinions of small-minded people.

Their throat convulses, and they wobble to their feet and clumsily rush down the carpeted theater steps and lurch out into the hall to flee to the nearest stark white bathroom stall.

Their knees hit the tiles, and what spills out of their mouth reeks and tastes of salty tears and phlegm and popcorn butter.

To make things even better, their nose prickles, and blood droplets fall into the toilet. What's most surprising is that someone has pushed the hair from their face. They aren't sure how Meph was able to fit into the stall with them.

When the demon helps them rise, their knees pop.

"I'm sorry." Soft as a calm breeze. Perse has never heard Meph apologize. They're even more unsure what to do when Meph takes a handkerchief—lined with gold thread, naturally—out of his breast pocket and dabs the blood off their mouth and chin. His expression is drawn, devoid of its usual sharp hint of snark. But Perse swears the skin under his eyes is damp.

With a wet sniff, Perse replies, "It's okay." No, it's not, but it is. Things aren't okay, but that's okay. "Were they..."

Were those real memories of when you were in Heaven?

Not just Heaven. The war. They see Meph alone, on the periphery of an immense garden, under a pomegranate tree. Lonely. Furious. Seething. His shimmering wings darkly red like blood. Pale nails dig into bark.

They can't complete the question, feeling its wrongness, its weight on both of their hearts.

—

That night, as the last of the late summer crickets scream before dying, Perse pulls the covers on their bed now. It's still warm enough to not need a quilt. And if Meph is in bed, he's like a self-sustaining heater.

They don't even need to ask Meph to come; he slips into bed with them, and they rest their head on his shoulder. His heat spreads against their cheek like wings, and Perse dozes, thinking about an old, distant shore.

MISERY IN COMPANY

Morgan Dante

Content Warnings: death, mention of offscreen violence

IT'S ABOUT TEN YEARS BEFORE the demon Mephistopheles burns an elderly couple alive for his lover, and before said lover collapses on the rheumy ocean's edge and dies.

Mephisto doesn't know this, and if he were to know now, he wouldn't care. He will win his bet against God and secure his prideful scholar's soul. That's all. There are no other stakes.

And he and Heinrich Faust aren't lovers yet.

He thinks about that last soul ripped to shreds by demons, the man's tongue in the fountain, twinkling teeth wriggling amid the ripples, an untethered eye rolling between softening crabapples.

The memory doesn't make him laugh; no, he doesn't feel anything. Feelings are for Heaven, with the demure but beautiful legions of curly-haired men idling by orange and pomegranate trees, strumming their harps and lazing about, conversing about nothing of importance in a way that, to them, has utmost importance.

The smiles, the held hands, the blushes, the kisses amid beds of roses, carnations and poppies pouring forth like torrents of blood, reeking of flower-musk and spicy cloves and cosmic tears.

Stern Gabriel writing down notes, fidgeting Raphael looping his fingers around his flute, flaxen-haired Lucifer opening his pretty pink mouth to sing.

And then right there by the persimmon tree was always nervous, stupid, insipid Mephisto wringing his hands because all he wanted to do was join his brothers, but if he failed, if he fumbled, it might ruin him. They'd laugh at him.

No, he didn't care, and it didn't matter. It doesn't matter, and it never does. Not when one of his younger brothers crumpled into cinders beneath his burning hands (i don't care), and not when his beautiful vermillion wings molted away (i don't care). The pain in his bones never truly departed after his fall (idon'tcare).

It doesn't matter.

If all is ordained, he would never care because it would do nothing. All he could do was approach the universe as a cosmic joke and take delight in human fumbling.

Leave the caring to God, who loves all, except for him.

That evening, Heinrich asks his devil to walk with him by the sea. Sand crunches under their boots.

The wind disturbs their dark overcoats, acrylic streaks in the gray haze before a storm. The water is eerily calm, its foam lightly tumbling over crushed seashells that glint like glass.

Heinrich stands a foot and a half shorter than Mephisto, and where Mephisto is thin as a rake, the former scholar has a small pouch of a belly under his white tunic. Though he still has a head of dark brown hair, there are thinning gray strands at the crown of his skull. The demon slides his hands into his trouser pockets while Heinrich, closest to the ocean, dreamily gazes out into the horizon with those watery blue eyes.

You are getting old, my little scholar. It's pathetic, but Mephisto can't explain how forlorn the idea of their time on the mortal coil coming to an end makes him. What will he do back in Hell, listen to Asmodeus boast about the latest palace orgy, watch Leviathan wriggle their tentacles around, sigh as the Minotaur gores another soul?

Boring, as usual.

Heinrich rubs his hands together as cold breath plumes from his nose and mouth. "Does the sight of the ocean at twilight rouse nothing in you?"

"No. It's a phenomenon that happens every day."

"Does the devil truly care about nothing?" Heinrich asks him. "Some might say the opposite of creation is destruction; I never thought destruction would be dispassionate. Even Hell doesn't sound devoid of feeling."

How to describe Hell? Absence of Heaven. Absence of God. In his more dramatic moments, he might even say that his existence right now is Hell by virtue of not being Heaven.

"The opposite of God's will is the lack of action. He cared enough to create. I don't. He created sin, suffering, and Hell, eventually. If we use an art metaphor, art often requires passion."

"Not always," Heinrich replies simply, "much of the greatest art created was done on commission. But what if you did make something? What does a damned creature have the urge to create?"

Mephisto says haughtily, "I've made you a lord. I think that suffices."

Then, they stop walking as Heinrich faces him. The man's disposition is unusually calm. "Is that what I am, your art to make? I don't seem to recall you crafting me with your strokes. If you've changed me from what I was, the melancholic professor and doctor, I'd say you've unmade me, instead."

"Perhaps. Most of creation has, in many areas, unraveling and unmaking. Decomposition to enrich the soil."

"If we follow your devil-logic, you've created me like God created everything, even the damned angels like you. And He did it out of love."

"I suppose. It's been so long since I was connected to God, even when I've spoken to Him in Heaven, that I've forgotten. I remember all else, except His love." All that remains is smoke, ashes, screams. The sizzling hollows where dead angels' ruined faces used to be.

Loving and being loved. Mephisto remembers an all-consuming jealousy and possessiveness, but not love in Heaven. Maybe it's this mental barrier where he cannot entirely recall God's voice, even if he remembers His words. Or perhaps the demon never understood, never acted like the other angels because he might end up looking stupid and insipid if he indulged in kisses.

Heinrich flashes a strangely soft smile that makes the demon, for the first time since he saw his companion disappear into the crowd at Walpurgisnacht, curious about the man's intentions. "Come, Mephisto, I want to see the ruins on the hill."

With that, Heinrich reaches out for him, a silent invitation, and without thinking about it, Mephisto grasps his cool hand.

They are up on the hill in an instant in the center of the long-crumbled temple with its decapitated pillars, which jut around them toward the swollen harvest moon like pearlescent bones. The moon, the stars, and the lazy penduluming of fireflies illuminate the stretch of ancient ruins. They are still facing one another, Mephisto elegant pianist's hands wrapped around Heinrich's.

Eternally, proudly nonplussed Mephisto startles when Heinrich takes his free hand and grazes a warm thumb against his cheekbone.

Mephisto tastes Heinrich's pulse in his wrist, his soul: salt; smoke; copper; grief; stubborn wonder.

"I've been wanting to mention something to you," the mortal man tells him.

The demon can only reply with his usual sardonicism. "Was the beach not discreet enough? Go on, then."

"When I was going to overdose on opium, you were the only one there for me." Mephisto remembers the tall glass of brown laudanum. A bitter solution indeed in that dim vaulted tomb Heinrich deemed a study. Dusty leatherbound texts and a skull. "And in the form of a massive poodle, no less." A huff before Heinrich's features soften. "You stayed with me. If you hadn't, I wouldn't be here. I wouldn't have seen all the grand sights you've shown me. With all the shadows that clouded my mind, you've been like sunshine to me."

The fool. *If you hadn't let me in, you wouldn't be doomed to go to Hell. I only follow you to wait for the moment your soul is ripe.*

Mephisto scowls. "I didn't do it for charity, darling."

Somberly, Heinrich replies, gaze half-lidded, "I know." With that, they both drop their hands to their sides as a thoughtful frown crosses the man's features. "Funny, I think that's the only time I've seen you annoyed. Bothered. I never thought I'd take it as an accomplishment to bother anyone."

He despises that Heinrich thinks that he helped him.

I've helped you into eternal damnation. I've proven God wrong. I haven't saved you. The devil doesn't save. I've made you mine, and through contract alone, I'm yours.

Is that true? After all, didn't the torments of Job, rotting with ruptured welts and crying out his dead children's names, offer him salvation and a deeper understanding of God?

The force that in doing evil does good. How remarkably droll. God could really be so predictable.

This time is different. Heinrich shows no signs of regretting his path or lamenting his future. There certainly isn't any regret when he rises on his toes and brushes his lips against the demon's. His mouth tastes of tartly sweet wine and potato soup with chives, mingling with sea salt and brimstone, all clashing with that constant undercurrent of blood.

When Mephisto pushes back, his tail lashing back and forth behind him, it feels like an act of violence, of claiming. Heinrich returns his shove, their tongues colliding, by reaching up to the back of Mephisto's head and taking fistfuls of Mephisto' long, silvery curls in a delightfully forceful gesture.

All Mephisto had wanted Heinrich to do was embrace seizing what he wanted and, in turn, falling into indulgent sin. He meant more creative ambitions like their romp in the Underworld and less becoming entangled like this. Sex, too, could become boring when faced with the repetitive futility of the cosmos. That really killed arousal.

Not that he's complaining about present events.

When they pull apart, the man's lips are already swollen.

Breathily heavily, Heinrich rasps against his ear, "Take us back to the house. To the bed."

Within a second, they're by the bed, and Heinrich shoves them on to it, and they tumble on the linen sheets. The room smells of tallow and old books.

Mephisto spreads his legs while, above him, Heinrich cradles his jaw—he seems to like doing that—and presses his open mouth to the demon's brow.

In good humor, Heinrich says, "You did make fun of my fumbling when I first met. God of Flies, I'm curious how much you watched me with my former lovers before you strutted into my life."

Biting back, the demon replies, "Oh, I don't know what you mean, but you realize that it takes a certain amount of stamina to be with an immortal lover. Eternity is a long time to perform."

Not dissuaded, Heinrich's hip grinds against his.

"I hate you sometimes," the man says, and their next kiss has teeth.

All of Heinrich's past lovers have died, so it might be some solace to share a bed with an immortal creature.

There won't be salvation. He must make sure of it.

He must prove to God that he will win Heinrich's soul.

He won't be in Heaven, kissing his old lovers. He must remain with me. In Hell, together.

That's the good thing about Hell: If misery loves company, you're never truly alone.

—

Predictably, the mortal man grows older.

Heinrich complains about his back aching and hip locking when he sits on the sofa or at his writing desk, and then he complains about being a lord because he must answer to so many when he once stayed locked inside. Mephisto crafts a silver, opal-studded staff and complains about a rube in the village stumbling while pants-pissingly drunk and vomiting on his fine boots, the ones with the ornate gold buckles.

The man thrashes in bed more often, enraptured by nightmares. More than once, Mephisto frowns when he sees the name that begins to form on Heinrich's lips, and he sets a slender hand on the man's cheek and whispers softly. The man releases a soft sob but seems to relax as the demon comes closer.

Do you know that you purr like a cat in your sleep? Heinrich asked him once, like he once asked if Mephisto knew that, besides brimstone, he also smelled of carnations. *It can be quite relaxing.*

I don't know what you mean, the demon replied. *I don't sleep.*

One clear morning, Heinrich frowns as, standing outside on the grass, Mephisto idly tosses a human skull in the air, the one Heinrich kept on the bookshelf in his old study.

"Whose skull is this?" Mephisto asks. "Poor Yorick the gravedigger?"

Dryly, Heinrich replies, shadows from poor sleep under his eyes, "Yes, that was his name."

With his fingers grooved into the eye sockets, Mephisto gives a mock gasp, presses the skull to his heart, and falls to the ground. Soon, with a shake of his head, Heinrich joins him to stare at the blue sky.

He's close. So close to proving God wrong, and then, he can retire to Hell with Heinrich. Despite everything, despite the brimstone and drama and cosmic implications, it sounds rather romantic.

The first spring of their love affair is the easiest. Mephisto grows to like the quaint little seaside cottage.

A year becomes two, and then a decade, and then another. Mephisto is always there, following Heinrich. And then, the man rubs the crust out of his eyes and complains that he can no longer read by candlelight because his vision is poorer. Then, with each passing month, he can see less and less.

Over the passing years, Mephisto cannot believe himself when he makes plans in his head of where Heinrich will stay in Hell; he'll ask Asmodeus if there's a spare room in his spacious golden palace. Before, he told himself that he didn't care about the ultimate fate of the soul in question post-damnation. All he cared about—all he had—was Heinrich's damnation because it meant he'd win his wager with God.

Eventually, Heinrich, almost without a wisp of hair, becomes thin, shivering when he's not under a mountain of quilts.

In the evening, the living room dim, Heinrichs sits on the seafoam-colored sofa with a large bowl of potato soup with celery and carrots on the coffee table. He takes the bowl in his hands and stares out into space with milky cataracts, his hand shaking violently around the spoon. Some of the soup spills on the blanket in his lap.

Mephisto comes over from the kitchen and sits beside the man, taking the bowl and the spoon. He raises some of the soup to Heinrich's lips, and Heinrich accepts, indignantly swallowing.

Heinrich grouses, "I know how to feed myself."

The demon only regards him steadily. "I know, Heinrich."

Despite his brief arguing, Heinrich lets Mephisto feed him and clean his chin with a gilt handkerchief. And after, when he huffs and fumbles with the brown laudanum bottle, Mephisto reaches for it and says, "Here." Heinrich lets him have it, but rather than fully taking it, Mephisto wraps his grip around Heinrich's and helps bring it to his lips.

Heinrich doesn't thank him, nor does he complain further, which unsettles Mephisto more than he'll ever admit. They've done this particular routine of medicine-giving for about two-hundred days. Two-hundred and twenty-three.

The man falls asleep against him. As he snores, Mephisto wraps his tail around him to keep him close.

Yes, this man is his. God, that jealous, tempestuous God, has no right to him.

—

Sitting on the sofa with a knitted blanket in his lap, Heinrich might not be able to see, but nevertheless, he stares in Mephisto' direction in abject horror, while the demon stands by the front door.

"You set them on *fire*?"

"Well, yes," Mephisto replies. "You can tell by the smoke in the distance."

Earlier in the day, Heinrich had been rubbing his hands and pacing. When Mephisto asked why, it was because the man had learned there was an elderly couple residing in a shed on his land without his consent because they didn't anticipate any punishments; Heinrich had always been a lax and forgiving lord.

Forgiveness doesn't exist in Hell.

Heinrich slumps down. "Here I am, cursed with you, unable to make things right. To care for myself without..."

Mephisto' hands fly to his chest, caged over his heart. "*I* take care of you, you ungrateful cretin."

"Yes, you've taken care of me, in more ways than one. You've done me in, like you helped along Gretchen's demise."

The demon prowls closer, crossing the distance to surge forward and trap Heinrich in the center of the sofa, striking out two hands to touch the back of the sofa.

"Get away from me," Heinrich hisses.

"Fool. You can't take responsibility for your actions, can you?" Moving one hand, Mephisto jabs a finger into his chin in mock contemplation. "I didn't drive the sword into her brother or offer her the sleeping potion that killed her mother. Unless I'm conveniently forgetting if I've ever possessed you, and why would I, when my form is exquisite? Her grief led to her disposition, and you are a walking monument to it."

"You're right. It was all my fault. I never should've left her alone with the child while she was grieving. I should've freed her from her cell instead of fleeing with you for this farce of a life."

"Yes, marvelous. And then she could've lived with you in your dingy little home as she squeezed out your pups, and then she could clean your ass. The woman truly died too soon."

Much quieter than the crackling hearth, Heinrich tells him, their faces an inch away from each other, "You are my servant, devil. So, I have instructions for you. Tomorrow morning, you will fill the coffee with all the opium in the house. You will serve it to me. And then, you will guide me to the shore."

"You don't need me to guide you."

"You will do it."

"Is tomorrow when you want to stop living?"

"I stopped living when Gretchen died."

Mephisto releases a rumbling laugh. "Oh, please. *Gretchen*. She was a silly, overly pious girl who went mad the moment you let her fall pregnant and 'manage' the new babe on her own with a pillow. She—"

Heinrich palms the blanket in agitation. "Don't."

"She did nothing for you but offer a distraction until you gained some sense and fled your dull little village. Done you in? I made you. No one else was strong enough. Patient enough." Mephisto gives him a rueful smile. "I've done everything else. I bathe you. I dress you. I put you to bed. I help you to the commode. Who made this blanket for you, again? You stupid, idiot, mortal man. I've done everything you asked of me and more."

"I didn't ask you to kill two helpless elderly people."

"What are those two near-dead, decrepit fools compared to what I've given you? I spared you from worrying about punishing them. If I hadn't done that, your land would be overrun with those eager to pick away and pick away until you have nothing."

Heinrich's jaw hardens. "I'm not arguing with you anymore."

Oh, please, it had to be a lie. All they've done for the past thirty years is argue.

Mephisto shifts away from Heinrich and straightens to his full height. "Suicide. All this wind, and you still want to ensure you go to Hell."

Chin lowered, Heinrich murmurs, "No. It won't be suicide. Merely an overdue consequence, the second half of a tragic love story."

The demon scoffs. "Oh, how beautiful. You too were truly starcrossed."

He can't logically reason why it bothers him that Heinrich still hasn't let go of that woman. After all this time. After all they've done. This is a human thing, surely, ruminating incessantly on the past.

And yet, what do fallen angels do but sigh and ruminate on old wrongs?

Tears spring to the old man's eyes. The demon hopes he doesn't start crying; he's always found crying to be tedious, so he hasn't done it himself since the Fall. "Stop. You've done a great evil, and in doing so in my name, I'm tarnished."

"Yet, my *tarnishing* of your oh-so-chaste soul—and your tarnishing of quite a few places of mine—hasn't bothered you until now. Everything I did to you, all those who died along the way so that you may retire by the sea and dine on lobster, hot soup, and chocolate cake, only now do you spurn me."

"Either way, I know I won't be alone," Heinrich says. It isn't self-reassurance; it's resignation. He whispers the final words: "No matter how much I hate you."

In the end, the man shuts his eyes. Glowering, Mephisto storms out, the air smelling faintly of curling smoke as one end of the blanket smolders.

—

After Heinrich takes all the opium, he stands by the ocean, and so does Mephisto, watching that cool resolve on a man so often moved into emotional overtures and worries about the state of the universe and the purpose of life.

Despite himself, despite his rage at Heinrich's defiance or the fact that they both know he'll be with the mortal, his mortal, until the end, despite his desire to let the idiot collapse alone with the weight of his own guilt and self-righteousness—

When Heinrich collapses, Mephisto is there to catch him, wrapping his arms around the man's shuddering body, feeling the hard surface of his head knock against the demon's collarbone, Heinrich's heartbeat sluggish.

He's there. When Heinrich falls, and when his heart stops. When the sky opens, and just as he's about to summon other demons to assist him with the transportation of Heinrich's soul, he's struck by visions of rose petals raining on the water and sand and a league of beautiful men with deeply golden skin and flowing tresses. All he wants is to kiss them, to be with them.

A lightning strike of pain seizes him, and when he comes to his senses, open flowers of blood spiral on his skin, and Heinrich, both his body and soul, is gone.

He was saved, and the only proof of the aftermath is Mephisto, alone.

Heinrich hadn't spoken a word to his demon that morning. His last words needed no elaboration.

I hate you.

The demon curls into himself on the sand, skin stippled from face to toe in bleeding sores. The saltwater crashing into his body only stings, his wounds sizzling as he cradles his face in both hands. How long will it take for anyone to find him? Eventually, he'll need to go to Hell and admit...

"Who do I have to complain to?" he asks no one.

He has nothing. He is nothing.

Rain trickles down his face.

This is who he always knew he was.

In turn, nothing has changed, as the devil never changes. His purpose remains the same. He'll go on as before and try to find another soul to trick.

ENFLESHED

Cas Trudeau

Content Warnings: internalized gender dysphoria, discussions of gender self-actualization

*"He lights, and to his proper shape returns
A Seraph wingd; six wings he wore, to shade
His lineaments Divine"*

- Milton's Paradise Lost, Book 5 lines 276-278

You tower, crown'd in meridian sun,
in that pasture before your bower;
sky sweet exhalations – that fragrant ambrosia
sipp'd upon by the fatherly orb –
coaxing thistle and weed into dance.
Amongst those yellow pillowed-petals
and violet bristle stalks, you search
for your own shadow. Quiet disciple,
he follow'd prostrate throughout the morn.
His coole touch clung as you tender
hand life from loam, midwife earthe into bloom.

Upon your shoulders, noon's heat mantles –
and shadow shivers. You wound
way to rib and rest, gulled within
your firm form. You retire alone,
caught cold atop mossy
maiden-bed. Eve awaits,
repose within nuptial narthex.

Her fingers curl, knuckles knead'd earthe;
her nails flutter as monarchs do, moon faces
perfect pink in their beds. Her honeysuckle hair
curls and clings to chest, sweat damp tresses
tinseled with twigs and leaves. When you gulf
upon this gifted shore, her guise shifts. Quiet
melody thrums though her teeth as she smiles,
eyes chariot along the horizon of your face.

She counts your eyelashes, your freckles,
those very particles of star and dust
bodies are built of. She shall know
you as your shadow does – for she
is of your clay. Yet, she drifts,
sole satellite in your orbit; a phantom
ache in your caged chest; longing throes
as you wonder – *what we would be
should she be of me and never leave.*

You lay in gift'd hatch, trek
canyons carv'd within your palms.
Hymn hums in your atrium chest,
sinew strung tight as fates' golden thread;
silence springs saliva in your mouth,
sour taste pooling upon your tongue.
Your hyacinth curls wilt
upon scorched cheeks, bones buzz
with cicada song. Tree limbs lumber
in the wind, tear satin sky
with needl'd hands. You wait on the eve,
with bat'd breath and prickl'd skin.

Light lingers behind mirage curtains –
a veil'd apparition beckoning you
from coole cradle. Shade weighs waxy
upon your spine, buried in
borrow'd cerement. You crawl
from this embosom, body plow'd
by root and stone. You kneel,
wrung with sweat in mire,
tarnished and blistered and *human*

when radiance strikes –
severs sky and sphere;
and divinity arrives.

You, Author of All, gift'd a name
for heav'nly stranger: *Raphael*.
You think to bowe, supplication
ceas'd by effulgent palms
upon your trembling shoulders.

You heard cherubic choirs at birth,
tast'd prayer's potent nectar. You danc'd
under newborn nebulas as celestial
bodies waltz'd across a galaxy's palm –
Yet, your heart has not once sung.

To look upon sun's façade
is to expunge all darkness
from one's earthly sight –

New dawn smiles upon you;
Raphael eclipses your jaw,
graces you with a greeting
of their lips. Eden envelop'd
in their world-wide wings,
golden swathes of down darn'd
with constellations unnam'd.
Raphael rests upon the threshold
of you, quenches your lungs' roots
with brisk ozone, sweet sharp
along tongues. Their teeth
scythes your lip, split harvest
from this pit of a mouth –

Summer shine ruptures, all swallow'd
you raptur'd in their embrace,
divinely devour'd, body burst,
bloomed, built beyond HIS
image. Adorned flesh sculpted
into Spirit –

you, bitten and bruis'd fruit, holy.

SWARM BEHAVIOR

Aurélio Loren

<u>Content Warnings</u>: sex, body horror, vague mentions of sexual assault, gore

SEEING PEOPLE HE KNEW at the strip club was one of his worst fears. At the sight of a recognizable curved nose and deep laugh, Jesse ducked into the back rooms, where some of his coworkers were adjusting their makeup. His heartbeat was heavy in his chest, thudding through his mind as he tried to collect himself. The back room had a cloud of perfume around it, masking the locker room reality.

"What do you do when you see someone you know?" Jesse prompted his coworkers, sitting down for a reprieve of his heels.

"Mm, an ex? That's the worst," Honey, who had hair to match, responded. She laughed seeing Jesse's frown at being read so easily. "Usually I flirt with another guy, show 'em I'm at work, they can't just bother me."

"Yeah," another girl started between swipes of lip gloss, "and always charge him extra," she paused to smack her lips together, "'specially if he asks for a dance."

He couldn't have told you how he got there. The forest was unfamiliar, he was sure of nothing but the unfamiliarity of it. Leaves hung off the branches and leaned in close, poison on their tongues and dreams in their whispers. The plants he could recognize seemed different, there was something off about them. Mugwort, the source of the reverie, leaning in close he was greeted with the small budding of flowers. The silver on the underside of the mugwort leaf was tinted a strange baby blue. Jesse attempted to rub it between his fingers, to reveal the trick. When he was unsuccessful, he continued quickly, ducking to the side and coming upon a grove of trees.

Fig trees, their palmate leaves reaching out to him, an unnervingly bright green. Fruiting, it could not have been the season, he plucked one from the branch. The thin skin of the fruit was tender between the pads of his fingers, overripe and shifting in his palm.

A wasp snapped its way through the flesh of the fruit, vibrating under the bruise colored skin, struggling with its newborn body. Fresh pinchers shredded pieces around the wriggling body. Dropping the fruit in horror, Jesse watched the wasp continue its birth of consumption. The sweet scent of rot followed him.

"Jade is a pretty name, think of it yourself?" His mouth turned up at his joke, his legs spread as wide as they could.

Jesse leaned forward, each of his hands grabbing the side of his chair, and he let the strange man stare at his chest as he whispered, "You sure you can keep up?"

The stranger grinned at this and Jesse could feel the man he knew stare at his back. The stranger in front of him reeked of broke but Jesse pulled a drink out of him. Sitting up straighter with a giggle and twirling the straw between the ice in his drink, Jesse felt himself transform.

The joints of his shoulders moved under his skin, they rolled and coiled, as if they were practicing. The sensation of his bones moving freely of his mind only had a moment to give him pause. The tearing sensation came back with a vengeance, he fell forward, his back hunched over, screaming into the soft ground. The dewy grass swallowed his screams and dirt packed itself underneath his nails as he scraped the ground in pain. A phantom pain, the blood rushing directly under his skin, eager to be freed.

Jesse's body moved to his choreography automatically, a familiar dance he had practiced so many times. A fan kick, his core tightened and his legs, his long muscular legs straddled out for the audience to watch, before Jesse climbed to the top. The bruise was already beginning to form against his thighs as they held him up against the cool metal pole. He spun and spun, his arms free to move outstretched as he floated above the ground. Fingertips spread out, in the flurry of movement, he could mistake them for wings. With one fluid move, he lifted himself up and, arms wrapped around the pole, he leaned back, able to hold his leg, contorting his body into a grotesquely beautiful shape. He spun and spun, eyes focused on the neon sign above the bar, in bright green, each turn his head caught the sign, held onto it for a moment, and spun once more. Jesse made his descent to the ground, falling, falling, falling like an angel from grace.

    Allowing the pole to split him in half, he grasped the cool metal with both hands and picked up his legs in a straddle, hitting his heels against each other with a smack. Twist. The pole was cold against his back as he slowly slid down, one leg stretching in front of him as he made his way to the floor. Back arched with a deep breath, his eyes focused to see the distorted faces, he could feel his body move with ease and flow. Almost without a thought, he rolled slowly to his stomach and lifted his hips in time with the beat, his ass moving and his hips circling, he could feel a few fleeting bills against him. Hungry eyes ate at him, consuming each piece of muscle and meat he had on display. They paid for the ability to sink their teeth into his smooth skin, ripping a chunk out to chew on. They left him dead and bloodied every evening on the stage, covered in his own sweat and the lingering smell of rubbing alcohol. As the song faded into silence, the eyes grew bored and he scrambled to pick up the bills that covered the stage, his fingers suddenly clumsy and awkward.

    The wiry grass left criss cross impressions on his knees, still shaking and unable to hold his weight. One hand reaching out, twisting, his fingers curled at the desperate hope of strength. The calluses on his hands cracked and dead skin fell to the earth. His fingers tore at the dirt beneath him, desperate for an escape. All of his acrylics had cracked off, splitting his nails, bloody, torn, and jagged. The nerves on his fingers revolted against being brought to light, searing pain flooding through him. It was once he had fallen, his body finally caving to the pillowy dirt. His cuticles. The soft thin moons that crested his nails, they began to pull, pull back. An invisible hand held them in its grip and tore. He screamed, for a moment the sensation brought a satisfying peel before it gave away to pain, the delicate skin of his fingers being flipped and torn from his skin, blood trailing down in thin, jagged lines. He watched in a frozen horror as strips of his skin, thin and dead, fell off of him and floated to the ground. The earth sensed the dead skin and the moss rolled over it, taking it as a price paid. The silence that followed his screams was deafening. The forest seemed to absorb all sound around it, the wide trunks of rough bark held onto the noise, keeping it sacred.

"Wait, you're J—"

Jesse cut off the familiar man before he could finish his sentence, his voice sharp, "It's Jade here."

The man understood and nodded.

"It's been a while," he spoke, his hands shoved in his pockets.

Jesse had not seen the man since they were so much younger. It felt like a lifetime ago. Jesse's heels almost brought him to this man's height—had he grown since they were young or had it simply been that long?

"I'm not here for uh— I'm— it's my friend's bachelor's party," he explained, making a point to make eye contact with Jesse, refusing to glance at the very skimpy outfit he was wearing. Jesse looked to where he had indicated. The man getting celebrated was clearly drunk, with multiple of Jesse's coworkers crowded around the man and his many friends.

"He looks like he's in good hands," Jesse remarked and the man laughed as if it had taken him by surprise.

"We should catch up," he blurted out, the words tumbling out of his mouth before he could catch them, clearly shocked by his own statement. Jesse studied his face, searching for something he couldn't quite place.

"Either you pay for the time or you wait until my shift is over," he strained his neck to look at the clock above the bar, "in three hours." It surprised Jesse how his stomach leapt at the sound of the man's deep laugh.

"If I buy a room can we just talk?" He took a last swig of his drink and put it down as Jesse took his hand and led him to a private room, where they sat next to each other, their bodies pressed close. The vague scent of sweat and beer filtered through the mask of perfume, assisted by the dim lights.

"It's been a few years," he chuckled, and ran a hand through his hair. It was greying some. "I uh, I haven't seen you since I left for rehab." he spoke softly, and Jesse couldn't move his gaze from the man in front of him, he couldn't recall if his face had always been so mature, stubble against his chin and weary lines pulling him down.

"Yeah, how've you been, how was that?" Jesse asked softly, wondering how it was possible to condense years into a few minutes. The man didn't have a chance to say goodbye to anyone before he was whisked into sobriety.

"It's uh, it's been an intense few years I guess." He seemed nervous and Jesse didn't know how to tell him not to be when he was still in his work clothes with most of his body on display. Usually having his chest bare calmed his clients. "Rehab worked I guess, although I'm not sure if I didn't just trade drugs for work. I guess that's just the normal way to outrun your problems." He laughed to himself, and halfheartedly gestured to his left hand. "I got married right out of rehab, I don't know, I think I uh—- wanted the stability."

Jesse's eyes grew wide and he nodded solemnly, like his story was unique. He had always been good at this part of the job—listening. Men paid for private rooms and spent half the time having their own therapy session. Jesse couldn't help but wonder what his wife looked like, how much she was privy to from his previous life.

"I work in a shitty office downtown where no one knows anything about each other but if I'm being honest," he leaned forward, his lips only inches from Jesse's neck and his voice quiet, "it all feels like a bit of a sham." The fabric of his shirt brushed up against Jesse's arm gently. The cologne he used was subtle and pleasant, earthy, he had changed it in the years they'd been apart. It lingered on Jesse's mind, he had kept the memory of his last cologne, one of the few parts of the man he could vividly remember.

Jesse found himself smiling quietly. He looked up at his old friend and his eyes didn't seem all that different from what Jesse had kept in his memories. They were still a soft brown, lighter on the edges and kinder the longer you looked at them. He had always remembered the eyes he had looked at Jesse with, and suddenly Jesse could barely remember why they hadn't stayed in contact.

chiiiurp, chiiiurp, chiiiurp. The sound followed him, a steady way to clock the seconds as they passed. Time faded away in the forest, slurring together until he could not tell the minutes from each other. His steps began to fall in line with their cries. Were they a warning? Or maybe a procession. A procession of one, being led deeper still into the trees. The tightness in his lungs refused to disappear and every breath raked nails against his throat. The clouds peeked through the trees around him, every step increased the elevation and his thoughts became less clear, the clouds creeping in, becoming more and more present. Each time he blinked, time began to slow and he allowed himself to lean into it causing his steps to fumble. His ankles, twisting, the bones being forced into awkward, unnatural angles, pressing against the skin, threatening to burst.

Even when he attempted to cry out, it came out pathetic and strangled, as though his voice had been plucked from him, pulled into the air around him.

He was taken back to being young. Jesse and the man had been in the back of a truck and trailer he had been hired to do deliveries. They were propped against the wall of the metal trailer, boxes piled around them, pushing them closer to each other.

"I still have a few deliveries," His voice dripped with desire as he spoke to Jesse, who straddled his knee and tucked some hair behind the man's ear as if he hadn't heard anything, "but we can go for dinner after," the man pledged solemnly and kissed Jesse's forehead and then his nose, then his lips. Jesse melted against him, the man's arms wrapped around his waist.

Jesse was intertwined with him, trying to convince him to skip the rest of his shift. Lips against the man's neck, he spoke covenants of devotion. His fingers traced universes into his back. Together, they slid to the floor giggling and smiling. The man rolled onto his back with a laugh of finality, and allowed himself to be swayed, the promise of pleasure too great.

Jesse's vision focused on a single green grasshopper, a sharper chirp as he hopped forward, slowly, towards him. Slow, consistent movements, with each leap, he noticed tiny changes. As the small insect's feet hit the ground his colors began to change. Green to a subtle yellow hue, creeping up his body. The exoskeleton began to harden and morph colors. The lines of veins pulsing, the fresh green began to fade to a soft yellow that crept up the bug's body. Jesse's palms pressed into the pillowy moss, a reprieve for his scraped palms, and pulled himself through the forest floor, scurrying away from the tiny insect.

"Like old times?" the man chuckled, leaning back into Jesse to taste him once more, desperate to reminisce. To fall into what could have been. Cramped in Jesse's parked car, they fumbled with their clothes, struggling to free themselves. They barely made it into a parking space before their lips were exploring each other. Jesse noticed the absence of a ring against his left hand, vaguely wondering if it'd been stuffed in a pocket and was now thrown against the ground. He moaned deep into his mouth at the thought. The man's fingers found their way against Jesse's thighs, drawing soft circles against his smooth skin. Jesse pulled at the man's hair, guiding him and desperate.

It was the way the insect crept so rhythmically towards him and seemed to cock its head as if it was staring. It was unnerving, his upper lip began to sweat and his arms began to shiver. The chirping grew louder, increasing slowly until it was a cacophony of desperate screams, all overlapping as if they were vying to be noticed. It took Jesse a while to realize his own screams had been added to the orchestra of pleas, his own throat raw until it began to bleed. The unmistakable sharp taste of blood ran down his throat as he gasped for breath. Air fought to make its way through his throat, he gurgled, realizing he was choking, dying on his own body.

"It wasn't like that, Jesse." His arms were wrapped around Jesse who forced familiarity to relax into the caress. The man kissed the top of Jesse's head and slowly raked his fingers through his soft curls. "I had to leave, I didn't have a choice," he murmured into Jesse's hair, his hands busy continuing to explore.

"I know," Jesse relented, his hands began to roam Jesse's back, feeling each ripple and fold. Jesse pressed his lips into the man's chest, his prayers of worship moaned into his flesh.

They began to swarm. He was waiting waiting waiting and once it began, it happened all at once. The color changes, the wailing, he didn't think it was possible for it to get more intense. He raised his arms in front of his face in a desperate attempt at protection as the bugs, oh god, the bugs, began to fly. Their wings thrummed together, a vibration that he could feel deep in his bones. Their tiny bodies shot by, too many, blocking his ability to see a path, thousands of them, the sky darkened by their masses. Their bodies crashed into his palms, their skeletons pulling his flesh down with them, their mandibles crushing into his skin, throwing their weight into attaching themselves to him and leaving gashes in a last attempt at cruelty. Jesse fell onto his back as he came to an understanding, the tension leaving his limbs and a mask of peace settling over his mind as he fell against the forest floor.

Jesse ground against the man in desperation, his nails tearing at the same back he had just allowed his kisses to take root. The man below him attempted to control the movement of his hips but he was clearly out of practice, his hands eventually settling against Jesse's chest and back. Honey poured out of Jesse and the man's eyes drank it up. Moans slipped out of him as he buried his face in the man's shoulder, slick with sweat, and he bit down against the flesh, and the man immediately replied with his own moan. It was only once Jesse's pleasure roared through him, his hands against broad shoulders, driving himself down, begging for his own release, that he allowed the man below to take his enjoyment. The man's hands wrapped around Jesse and they rolled over together, his lips grazing against Jesse's neck.

Tiny pieces of torn leaves fell against him and all around him, a rainfall for the death of a tree. He was surrounded by the beauty of decay. Jesse smiled against it, the vague thought of a death alongside the death of a forest. He would rot with them, the roots of the trees slowly pulled him into the soft earth. The crows, calling out as they gathered and pecked at his eyes. The foxes, scavenging, would take his fingers, running off with their spoils. Maybe the maggots would claim his tongue, maybe the hawk would find his liver.

But it was the caterpillars who began to congregate, as if he were at the pulpit preaching. Their tiny legs dotted against him as they began to drag silk across his body. It was a torturously slow process, his mind delirious as they bound fibers to each layer, thousands of them, of every species, from every part of the forest, coming to his call. Small neon inchworms darted across his face, their silk thin and strong, covering his mouth. Horned devils made a slow aggressive path up his legs, strapping them together. The leeches made their way towards his body, draining their fill of blood before creating a spongy jelly layer of their own. The creatures pulled themselves across him, claiming him as their own. Cocooned by the forest, he gave himself up to the way they encased him.

In the height of the man's ecstasy, eyes closed and his hips quick, he breathed out a single word, *"Jade"*.

Jesse froze underneath him, staring up at the man whose eyes were still shut with pleasure, his breath only just beginning to calm. He could not recognize the man suddenly, his face had changed and ice slid into Jesse's veins. It wasn't until the man opened his eyes and saw Jesse staring back at him blankly. It was only in that moment that he realized.

"No— I didn't mean." He scrambled, and the two of them sat up, there was only a few feet between them but Jesse made sure they were no longer touching. Their bare, glistening, bodies reflected the intimacy they had just shared and the distance between them began to grow.

Silently, Jesse pulled a t-shirt over his body. "Don't— hey, listen, no— don't." The man put a hand on Jesse's arm, trying to persuade him back into his arms. "I'm sorry, it was an accident," he tried once more, his voice pleading.

Jesse's shoulders sagged, he was so tired. Immediately he could feel a hand on his shoulder, and a voice that sounded muffled underwater, as if they had sunk deep underground.

"Please, let me explain—" The man's voice strained and suddenly became meek.

It was only at this point that Jesse spoke, "Explain what? What do you have to say?" The harsh words hung in the air between them.

"I— I'm— I didn't mean to— I meant to say your name." Defeat weighed in his voice and his shoulders hunched forward. He took Jesse's hand and kissed it tentatively.

"I would never mean to do that." He tucked a piece of Jesse's hair behind his ear, stroking his cheek with his thumb. "I feel so awful." His face had morphed back into something Jesse could recognize. Jesse held the man's hand against his cheek, closing his eyes for a moment, pretending it was kindness.

It began in his shoulders, under his skin. The ache refused to be ignored. He rolled his shoulders and his neck, exhaustion creeping up on him. He stretched his arms above him, his wrists twisting and crackling, his shoulders strained and tight. His hands touched the cocoon around him, tightly wound together. The air around him was thin, suffocating. The urge to panic had subsided, replaced by the irritation of pain.

It felt like an infection, running hot through his veins. His fingers dug into the skin behind his neck, clawing into his muscles desperate for release. The tissue disobeyed the restraints of his skin. There was no way to tell whether it was his fingertips burning or the skin beneath them, inflamed and furious. He curled his arms inward, turning to cradle himself on his knees, stretching the canvas of his back taut.

"I'm so sorry, forgive me," he kissed Jesse's hand, "forgive me," kissed his wrist, "forgive me," up his arm, "I missed you so much," his voice was husk by the time he made his way to Jesse's neck, his kisses becoming less delicate. "I'm such a piece of shit," he whispered into Jesse's hair. "You're so beautiful." The man slid towards him, wrapping his hands around his waist.

Jesse still stared forward, his hands loose around the man's back. Any thoughts he had were tangled, unreliable, he couldn't trust them. He rubbed the man's back slowly; the only sign of forgiveness the man needed. The man jumped on this moment and continued to eat at Jesse's neck, his fingers dipping into him, reaching for absolution.

He was molting, like the insects before him his shell began to detach as he grew anew. The skin seemed to have nothing to hold onto, loose on his back, only hanging on by his hunched figure. His capillaries had broken under his skin, one by one, bursting with a pop, blood running down his limbs. his veins and his arteries began to rearrange themselves, growing and twisting like a pit of snakes. Wriggling over each other in a confused attempt at creation. Fluid pumped through these new veins, awkwardly forming the shape of a dysfunctional wing. The case that held him so tightly began to crack. Veins curled and coiled around themselves, attracting each other like lost lovers. One by one his ligaments began to detangle themselves from his raw muscles, roping themselves together, his body began anew.

Howling in pain he curled up tighter, until all he could hear was the pounding of his heart and the tearing of his flesh, the ripping of skin echoed against the walls of his dark casing. His hands froze in mismatched crooked claws. The nerves on his back, raw and pounding, screamed in stimulation, he could feel them vibrating. It felt like years he spent cocooned, suspended in a vat of his own body's secretions as it began its rearrangement.

The drive back was more awkward than either of them would acknowledge. The silence between them seemed to extend past the music thrumming out of the car radio. Jesse hadn't planned for a guest in his car, last minute he had shoved the trash from the passenger's seat to the backseat floor, covering it with a few coats and a prayer, cheeks hot when he realized the man was chuckling outside his car peering in.

"Up here on the left," he spoke quietly, and Jesse silently parked in front of a normal looking townhouse. The man turned to face him and stared, waiting. Jesse refused to meet his eyes, focusing on the details of the house.

"I don't— this isn't—" The man took a short breath. Jesse ignored the hint of frustration in his voice. "I haven't done this before, okay?" The man searched Jesse's eyes and when he couldn't find what he was looking for Jesse watched the man huff, slam the car door, walk up to his house, straighten his shirt, and gaze up at the dark windows of his house. He fumbled with the lock and before he could look back, Jesse had pulled his car forward and rolled up his windows, out of sight.

His wings were new and so they were wet. The skin was the fresh pink of skinned flesh and striped with muscle and tendons, pulled into pointed taut wings. The remnants of his cage were in tattered pieces on the ground, held together by broken strips of silk. Dripping with mucus and slime they flapped unsuccessfully, only managing to pull Jesse upright. He tried to land his feet against the dirt but they crumbled against the new weight, his bones cracking and rolling. Yelping in pain, he tried to stay grounded but his wings demanded autonomy and once again yanked him into the air, feet suddenly pulled off the earth, he dangled uselessly.

Jesse attempted to go limp, wanting to be left alone on the ground like a child throwing a tantrum. It became increasingly clear he was not going to be given his wish and he groaned in frustration, the giant wings insistent on movement. Jerked into the air once more, he began to understand his balance, and how to navigate his body weight and his wings. When he shifted his weight his wings responded. Attempting to keep his body from shuddering with every breath became easier. With a triumphant yell, he unfurled his arms and palms, stretching them wide until his fingertips pulled at the skin, ripping at the wounds across his body. His ribs strained against his chest and he shot forward into the cool air.

Jesse turned into a side road. He had been aimlessly driving for what felt like hours. subconsciously making his way to an old hiking trail. He parked in front of the trail entrance, the trees overhanging, waving at him slowly. Jesse fished through his work bag, pulling out all the cash, propping his feet up against the dashboard. Inside was a small tin box that held a single joint, his reward for completing a shift. To get out of the club quickly he'd tipped out and left without counting his earnings.

Flicking open a lighter, he took a hit of the joint, sifting through the cash in his lap. He grinned and exhaled slowly, smoke covering the bills, his lips moved silently. He had up-charged the man. The smoke filtered through the open window, Jesse watched it creep up into the night sky and disappear into the looming branches.

With his rent payment in his lap, he sorted it once again into neat piles, matching the pile of ash that sat outside his car window. The night air coaxed him through his open windows, the cool breeze seductive. A whisper, brought through the wind, made its way to him, wrapping around his mind. Jesse looked deep into the darkened trailhead, the buzz of the insects pulling, pulling at his mind.

"Fuck," Jesse muttered just before his feet hit the tops of a tree, bark raking against his shin, leaving a trail of sap before it tumbled to the ground. He watched it numbly as it broke once more, the sound of shattering echoing around his mind.

The wings beat off time from each other and his legs dangled unceremoniously, like a child learning how to ride a bike. He teetered and swayed fifty feet in the air, less tentative of the night. Again, he leaned forward and without minding his balance, rushed into a large tree branch, he wrapped his arms around it, as his breath left him, desperate for a moment of reprieve. The rough bark dragged against his forearms, sap intermingling with blood. Heaving gulps of air, he began to understand the exhaustion that came with flight and freedom. With a final breath, he began off again into the night.

The man stared up at the monstrosity in front of him. He believed himself still in his dream; the knocking at the window had been incessant until he made the mistake of looking. In full view, he could just barely make out the remnants of his lover's face. Grotesque chunks of flesh hung off of him and it took the man a moment to understand they were wings. Terrible contortions of muscles and veins, pulsing through the thin flesh. They held up the remains of who he used to know, what he barely could recognize as the body he had worshiped just hours ago. He screamed, the sound hollow but the feeling taking his chest.

The man crawled away from him, as far up the wall as his feeble hands could take him, before Jesse swooped forward grabbing the man's neck in his grip. It felt so much smaller in his hands. He could feel the man's windpipe in between his fingers, slowly cutting off oxygen, each finger adding more pressure while the man squirmed and clawed at the arms that were already torn and flayed. It struck Jesse with hilarity that he could not feel the man's feeble attempts at freedom, it was a faded pain. He watched his arms spout blood but could not feel it. A grin peeled against his face, and with strength he did not know he possessed, he threw the man back against the bed. With a hand on either side of the man's face, frozen in a mask of horror, Jesse leaned down and playfully bit the man's ear.

The man whimpered and a hushed scream escaped his lips, the thing that used to be his lover looked at him with hunger in his eyes and he fell silent.

His teeth, had they grown sharper or had he just now noticed the way enamel tore through meat? Jesse ran his tongue over his teeth and the canines stabbed it. Just now noticing his gums throbbing, inflamed and red, Jesse tossed his head in discomfort.

Every cell in his body rioted for sustenance and he leaned forward, his lips parting slightly. Leaving a kiss on the soft skin in front of him, the vague feeling of nostalgia floating by, as he continued to leave kisses against the familiar body. He told himself it was another kiss, opening his mouth wider, allowing his teeth to sink into the flesh. The man was screaming differently than the last time they did this. It struck Jesse as odd, he had never heard the body below him call out like that. Teeth sunk deeper deeper into his skin. Tear. Only allowing his body to lead, he tore and was rewarded with an applause of wailing. It was as if the horrors he had fell to in the forest were forgotten from his body, with each swallow his scars softened. Every tear stitched together his own wounds. Every drop of blood fallen from the man replenished a drop of his own. Jesse gave in, falling into frenzy. Strips of muscles torn, the ripping of raw sinew hitting the walls with a dripping smack. Bones snapped and marrow sucked, he treated it as sacred, refusing to spill his treasure. Blood dripped from the ceiling. Onto the angel, the curls matted, falling against his face. He would be drenched soon enough.

The body was left in the room of horrors. With the call of dawn, the ants marched through. Trudging through the sludge, they pulled pieces of flesh for their own, spreading the word. Carrion beetles colonized to feast and start anew. Maggots, the true keepers of the gates, inspected their claims, wriggling deeper into the leftover flesh. The only movement was the larvae that were birthed into the rot.

RECOVERED CONTENTS FROM AN ANGEL'S STOMACH

Rae Novotny

<u>Content Warnings</u>: mentioned animal death & cruelty, bodily fluids, body horror, cannibalism, death, gore, strong language

ANGEL SUCKS ITS QUARRY'S TRAIL from thin air as a dogfish might swallow a string of plastic pearls, gaping, gagging, and pushing great swallows down its windpipe. After a minute of stillness, it convulses. Its gray skin goes paler still. Foam gathers at the corners of its colorless lips, and a fluvial stain pours forth from its mouth, separating into a crimson pall. Altostratus gas spills limp past under its reaching hand as it swings around and points along the path that its lungs have disgorged. Here—an apparition. A faint shape, a fugitive sitting on the roof's lip, formed of pheromone-laden perspiration: he's plump, human, and playing with a curl of his dark hair. He smells like salvation. If it weren't so hungry, Angel might've liked to find him, press its nose into his ample chest, and just *sniff* him.

But its stomach makes a painful sound, like a dead thing rattling its last in the pits of a storm drain, so Angel rolls its loose hand into a fist and punches itself hard under its ribs. A different dull ache replaces the first, and it rubs itself through anti-flak nylon as its dye dissipates into the wind.

Its fleshy mouth quivers, and flattens into a pathetic line.

This time, it's time—time for food.

High above hangs an abandoned sun. Fins of it fall through the city's upper floors, and wriggle out amidst ranks of constructions swaying in an oily sealskin of shadow. Cold descends across petroleum-stained magnet pads, and sirens howl in snatches of polar color. In the pits, acid rain is sluicing over the awning of a haircutting parlor, making opalescent orchids in the remains of a boulevard, and under that asphalt is aggregate; under the aggregate, more aggregate, so fine that it's almost soil; and under that soil, parking garages that sprawl for miles, deeper and deeper, until the parking valets resemble cavefish, and a sunken hush permeates the caverns.

Low: a pulse. Lower: it's louder. Lower, and faster through the hollows, until an antique car appears, coated in orange urethane paint, and polished to a flawless satin finish. Myriad spokes kiss its whitewall tires, and fruits and flowers styled like oil paintings crest its adorned hood. It's huge, and it's roaring, headlights pouring forth into cotton candy smoke rising from a silver undercarriage. Reverberations pummel concrete poles, which yank their graffiti stockings up against fingers of pinkish vapor. Up the hood, through dusky laminate, to the driver's face—he has a lipsticked mouth full of dove pinions, and a dehydrated tongue punched through with surgical steel, sliced in half almost to his missing tonsils. It's stippled with papillae, paler on the flat, ridged with molar-marks around the sides. He licks his lips and glances nervously at the shotgun seat. An aluminum tray sprawls across the upholstery, heaped with pulled pork all slid into one corner, and glistening with rivulets of hot grease.

He's never fed anything that wasn't a stray dog. Pork is supposed to taste most like human flesh, isn't it?

His hunter looks hungry. Privately, he thinks that if he got its clothes off, its ribs would look like grandstands.

Sworn dirt cages him. Worms squirm through contaminated soil, up, up, and up, and meet more garage walls lying under the first layer of what passes for dirt. Another road lies dead, and soda spills make sticky filth that accumulates cockroach antennae. Angel's strapped shoes pull up strings from the pavement. A grappling hook runs on rope from its leather plumage, and drags, sparking, along the road in its wake, past the span of its huge wings. Its right-hand fingers spasm around a four-muzzled catalytic mortar fastened to its other arm. Its glassy stare glows red, red as a Gonga lure's, stark above the hood of its mouth, as it follows a midair suspension, a scent floating in a medium of particulates, of droplets, and of pollutomatic filth. It's on high alert. Its abyssal stomach is churning, as if it's still flying in host with its littermates so far above. Nine months of this, and Angel feels its halo collaring its neck. Hunger scrapes infected nails along its stomach walls. It needs meat, ruined muscle, and sinew.

The fugitive should've killed himself while he had the chance. He is its fate. If he's killed, it's fed, and if he's not, it's—

it'll roadkill-doze on a kennel floor and dream of a man's apocrine glands: his underarms, his areolas, his—

and dream of concealment from cameras—

"Hurry up," the fugitive mutters. He looks at himself in the rearview mirror. After this long, it's like he can feel it getting close—its presence flutters in his stomach, and resonates in his heart. Fear, infatuation, or foresight? The fugitive's antique automobile, a 2049 Ormandy Resistor, shakes as his fingertips pass through suspended scarlet-and-menagerine controls and play up the ARR1 sound, a phantasmic cross of a feminine sigh and the Soviet probe Venera 14's 1981 recording of Venus's surface winds. He reclines, drills the sound into his head; raises his Resistor up, and drops it so hard his stomach comes loose. He looks at himself again, and pushes a fierce smile to the front of his face.

"All hidden things must plain appear."

And in the next moment, it does. It materializes in his smoky headlights— its arms, a mass of machinery, its shins, armored in Pantax, its neck, preternaturally long, and choked in a collar. Leather folds droop down its androgynous shoulders to meet ammunition-laden harnesses and a militaristically layered midriff. Lacerations mark the soft flesh of its upper thighs, naked, and lithe as a Saluki's. And its wings, its *wings*—sharp, and white, like immodest fangs. It's so much more gorgeous than he'd remembered. God, he thinks, is a pervert.

All the smoke is dematerializing, now. Angel faces off against the Resistor on a flat cliff. It's small and passerine, soaked in the car's headlights, and the Resistor's sole passenger is larger than life. Angel's white feathers fly in no wind. Its nostrils flare, and it raises its nose.

Pork?

The fugitive snatches the foil pan from the passenger's seat, and, with the pile of meat still warm on his callused palm, flings the driver's side door wide. His heavy car sways as one of his heeled riders hits precast concrete. Angel raises its quadruple muzzle mortar. Amaranthine light coalesces in crescents around the girth of it as it powers up, ringing with a charge that shorts the circuits overhead and makes an active windfall of sparks all along the room's rim. It's singing, gathering all of its light in its middle, like Holy Mary whispering a lullaby to the monster in its irradiated arms. Angel aims, and raises its spare hand to its mouth. It's salivating uncontrollably. Across from its gun, the fugitive catches his metal-riddled lower lip in his incisors. He dodges its first poorly formed shot. A hole forms in the wall at the room's furthest reach, and starts to piss out liquid matter.

The fugitive's smile curls his shout up at the corners. "You hungry?"

It gropes off another shot, and struggles to raise its gun again for its purpling skin. It groans. Recoil noise rings in its mind. There was a time, once, in which imprisoning an angel was an unthinkable feat, a crusade akin to reaching the moon in its opal asylum. How far away the planets must have looked to those people. First, the moon, last, the angels. To think he still might survive this—with such faith, this man might've finally reeled in time itself. Angel drools. Why won't he die as all the others did?

Angel looks up again to find the fugitive crouching with his cargo, slowly, as if he's still ready to run. A million metal spikes move on his clothes. He looks shattered. Sharp. Covered in mirrors.

He places the foil pan on a stripe of paint, and Angel's arms go soft. It wipes its mouth again, and saliva smears across its cheek.

He retreats a few paces. For a moment, Angel is too dull and doltish to answer. In the next, it makes a decision. It raises its shaking arm, and fires at his car. A pure shaft of foxglove light hits it at a diagonal, and dissevers the front from the rear. For a moment, the Resistor melts apart in slow motion. As purple disintegrates into dusky smoke, the fugitive covers his mouth with his hand, and his face swims from delight to sudden desolation.

He stands stock-still. Ahead of him, the car's internal components catch fire.

Angel drops its gun and dives hands-first at the foil pan. It falls upon the pork with abandon. It's past the point of relishing anything. It can't register flavor, or how the meat feels in its mouth. It is lost to need. It forces handfuls into its mouth, scarcely chewing. It feels more and more hollow the more it swallows.

"Is it any good?"

Angel can't recall time passing. The fugitive's metal-capped riders scuff the concrete a foot away. Firelight flickers on his shins.

"I'm not much of a cook," he says.

It swivels its head to look up at him. Its face is a mirage of grease, and its gun rests dead on the ground past its shoulder. A film of spittle rinses its canines and recedes to architraves along its gum as it snarls. It has strings of meat stuck in its piercing incisors.

"Don't glut yourself," he says, gently. "You'll get sick."

It doesn't heed him. It fits another greasy handful of pulled pork into its mouth, and gulps it down.

He crosses to its flank, crouches, and puts a hand on its shoulder. It ignores his slight pull, so he presses. It pays him no attention until he takes it two-handed, and pulls it away from the tray. In an instant, it's on him, its fingers around his neck. His head hits the line of a parking space with a *clunk* that nearly knocks him unconscious. He clutches at its sinewy arms as a small, armored hand chokes him, shutting off his airflow and forcing a small, pained noise from his mouth. His heart palpitates, and his pulse pounds in his skull. This close, he can count its lashes. Its nose is a mutilated flower around its nostrils, and its mouth, a dribbling slit. Its other features are so delicate and doll-like that it hurts to look at it for too long.

His hand falls from its arm, and he reaches up to stroke its hair. His periphery starts to pulse. Spots of nothing float in his sight as it lowers its face to his. It makes phonic snuffling sounds as it noses his cheek, his chin, and his neck, and he allows its chilly hand to move under his shirt, and across the coconut husk of his stomach. A soft "Hello" slips from his hardening lungs as it presses its face into his breast.

It inhales loudly—*'snnmsss...'*

He manages a husky little laugh, and its hand slips from his neck. It looks startled. He revels in the sudden sugariness of the air following deprivation.

"I have a home for you," he puffs, through his strained panting. "You remember what a home is? A nice, hot meal at night? Maybe a little more romantic than this?"

Angel sniffles. He can't understand how hungry it is. He hasn't felt hunger like this. If the natural use of immortal hunger is control, the natural consequence of immortal hunger is frenzied loss of it. Now that it's had meat, all it can think about is having more. And not only has it not fed in months—it hasn't had proper nourishment in an age. It feeds on what scraps of goodness it found in profane food and people. It's never enough. It hasn't really fed in so long, it's forgotten how divinity feels. It only knows that the fugitive's smell reminds it of manna...

"I can help you," he whispers, under its hands.

It attacks him with a single ravenous kiss. His neck is made of cords and cables, and it's sweaty, a little salty on Angel's lips. It pulls away, slowly, to look at the gaping hole it's made, and a horrifying noise flutters from the fugitive's slack mouth.

He doesn't look like he thought he could die. Fright like a doe's is large in his eyes. Angel mourns for him in this final moment of panic, in which a smaller person might feel peace.

Don't fear me, it thinks. *This was always your fate.*

He doesn't go quickly or quietly. He makes sounds for the longest time: fighting roars, piercing lathers of agony, and long moans as his organs come apart in strips and ribbons, cull and lace. He is uncomfortably hot in Angel's hands— huge on the outside, and small on the inside. His skin is slick. His red-striped palm reaches into the air, closing in. Smoke flavored with coolant mixes with his cruor. He groans, long and low.

I am Angel. I am a guide.

A room circles Angel like a millipede, and dismantled cubicles fill its corners. Dystonic lights hang from a cage roof. Angel squirms on a mattress stained with its own fluids, its strange face contorted in anticipation of pain.

"Is he dead, or isn't he?"

Angel whips its face to one side. A hand slices a cruel Y-shape across its abdomen, and peels its skin away in flaps. Angel resembles a Rhinelander rabbit, a little girl's vivisected pet—an animal with a cream-colored pelt, and soft spots of gray and fawn, dragging its guts along under it as it hops to its death.

"Damn it," a man snarls. "Pass me that—"

Angel's spine curves. It's crying and pleading in a language no one here understands. Gloved hands reach inside of it, hunting, searching. A flashlight shows glimpses of glistening places outside of this dimension, caverns criminal to the laws of physics, and folds of intestines too long for its abdominal cavity.

"That lump. Cut into it."

Angel screams and contorts. From out of its insides comes a thing at first shrunken, still bloating and blossoming into real size: the mangled remains of a human head. It has ruined cheeks, and fragments of skull under its missing nose, and it sheds flesh onto the gloves that hold it. Angel goes still. Half a face: a plump mouth, and pierced lips. Panic makes its hands limp, as frantic and clumsy as flowers flying in a spring wind. It pushes the peaks of its shoulders hard into the mattress, down, away.

"—really chewed him up—"

"—sure."

It was pleasantly full for a moment, and now it can hardly move. The pain of the instruments picking through its innards makes it shriek like a hyena. A huge face covered in a cold lilac lens looks down on it from above, and Angel imitates the fugitive's cry in reply. Maybe he is still the lucky one. How fortunate for him that he can go into darkness, into death, and find that pallid citadel of Angel's first small millennia rising up in front of him so fast. It howls as a hand slaps its face, and its manacles strain.

"Its halo. Its halo! Hold it!"

Hands circle Angel's neck, and it scalds them with its fury. It feels the coward recoil.

"—your calculations, you sniveling nutsack? You said—"

"It's too strong! Oh, shit. Oh, Lord have Mercy. Look at those wings unfolding..." A faint, cowardly crack. "Its *ribs*—it's like a fucking albatross!"

In a shattering instant, its restraints fracture and fall away. The fugitive's head starts to laugh. The white-coated figure holding it shouts, and fumbles it away from his chest. Angel reaches out for it as the walls close in, carapace-like, around its captors. It launches itself from the mattress that plunges and lists under its naked feet, and lands on all fours, ankles folding, wings flapping in short, useless strokes too large for the confined room. It forces the fugitive's head-half into its unfurling mouth and swallows it. Stars splinter in its scarlet pupils. White coats collapse in an avalanche to the floor, and red spots dot the fallen as Angel scrambles clumsily to the door.

It doesn't stop until it's outside, and it's finally ripped all its armor to pieces. It's nude. Sanguinary wings fall from its shoulders, arms, hips, and ankles, all dirty and soiled. Its hand slaps a windowpane. Ranks of portals rise up a stark wall: pretty windows full of lights, which mutate from dark, to dirge-purple, to orange rind, mango, and gold. Angel shoots past, all the way up to pure night. Its ascension pulls wind-fingers through its hair, dislodging chunks of its halo, now dark, its shattered parts still stuck amidst inky snarls. Dried filth flakes from its face.

It flaps, and carries itself for a hundred thousand miles. Manna, manna, manna—it's like it can't fall.

Above hangs a sun like a lemon, a clementine, cut apart. Angel struggles through an arid mesa on feet and ankles coated in gunpowder dirt. It's walking with a hand on its stomach—or, more hinging and hitching forward than walking, but fast, nonetheless. Fluids and pieces of the fugitive's chewed-up flesh coat its fingers. Its innards are still hanging out, still healing, but it's not those that it's so desperate to hold in: it's the fugitive, the rest of his head, his heart. It clutches itself harder. At this point, it could lose miles of intestines, and it wouldn't care. It's only this final impending separation that is unthinkable.

Constipation cramps fold it in half. It rises again, and staggers onwards. How much of him is fecal matter? How long can it last, without finding a way to follow?

Past Angel's sickly form, mesas rise and fall for miles, and finally reach a shoreline. As the sun slides down to the radioactive horizon, arcs rise and crisscross its formidable surface. Past the last line of the atmosphere, its modulation starts to sound automotive. Solar flares from late August, the roar of colliding metal; a self-perpetuating looping, humming, the calls from monsters of millennia ago; whistler waves, a high-pitched wailing, and farther, a low rumble announcing a car parked among the stars. Its driver has white dwarfs for his piercings. From the last sane reaches of lethal inhumanity comes a voice that moves like a shark, forever, with no start and no finish. Out here, meaning is only a short occurence in an inane sequence that persists for infinity:

"—go forth," it says, "and find my angel—"

The former fugitive grins. Flames shoot from his hood vents, all color in the cold necrosis surrounding him, and hot luminance licks his neck. Mankind might have ransacked the very pearly gates at last, if only he cared to share this course with any of them. He follows a roiling path of angels through the plexus of space, accelerating through time, and thinks of utter destruction at a single angel's hands.

Heaven at last: to be utterly devout, and devoured.

AN ANGEL SONG FROM THE ETHER

Rafael Nicolás

<u>Content Warnings</u>: Sexual Content, Some Violence

In the second circle of hell, they tell me,
the lustful live in a tempest,
hands outstretched, fingers caught
in the leaving breaths of their lovers,
never quite touching the fleeting, wind-swept
bodies — once familiar chests, rising, falling
— the press of love becoming memory, becoming
unremembered, the budding stranger
of your lover in leviathan hurricanes
the Lord has damned you to chase love in
until the end of time

But hell is also on earth,
and the lustful have brought their storm,
the winds that drag them from canyon to sea;
watch and catch them falling and flying
when a breeze flings them toward the sun only to
plunge them into deep dusk again; they scratch at the sky, picking
at stars, startling them; the lovers, wanting to grapple each other in
the eye of the hurricane — for a second's serenity —
reaching with their mouths, not their hands,
their tongues flicking out at the ether
between them

See the first lovers, the forth-bringers of this hell —
the beautiful devil, ensnarled in sun-threaded hair, in
upturned nose, in snaking twirls to cherry lips, and arrogant sighs,
and the archangel, wrestling the winds, striking feathers to
beat his body until the incarnate of it is brought to ember;
sweet angels, pray for these damned souls, torn askew by the tempest of lust

Yet here I will tell you a story I shouldn't:

The devil says, I let myself fall,
believing you'd catch me,
but our archangel has not spoken in centuries;
the chief prince, half dead, but never dead,
the angel, taking now his sin by the waist
like he should have done at the dawn
of creation, when they were cut from the same tendon of God,
blown from Him, like runaway pollen, seized from His womb,
the gore of the ether itself

Let the first lovers struggle against the whirlwind and
become the body of the hurricane,
the beast of the end,
a rapture of somber demons remembering
to sing again
in the last moments they can

They tell me the heart can cave in,
angels, but the adversary of God brings an open
embrace to the prince of heaven, a seraphim
with all six wings still and the very sun gathered at his halo;
lingered love, overstayed and unwelcome, yet
they introduce themselves again,
in the hell they've made, of this beautiful earth

The tempest of sin loses its teeth and out comes
the deep red from its mouth; but, Lord, the damned
cannot fear damnation, and the angel and the demon —
they say, We will make, of hell, a paradise,
I will find paradise,
unearth it from you,
by prying you apart and tugging you free,
from the binding of your anger,
now so ancient it has become something else, this
exhaustion

Devil, delicate and kind monster, let me
wet you with my mouth, as if I were
introducing you to God, my Lord, and
dipping you into blessed water, days after birth;
fallen angel, I have you now at the end of time,
and in your lovely, vicious heat, my coaxing fingers at your
gate, I think there is hell, inside of you

Angel, I waited long enough for you, there
is no love left in me, now, but lust I've never known
to live without, so grip my thighs and feel how they're
soft where they ought to be held firm enough the pain
overcomes the pleasure; my hips shiver up into the
air, and you take them, and you, shy, put yourself up against me,
and I ask, Will you descend from your Father's house and stay
in the storm with me; if you will, I'll part my gate and invite
you inside, allow you to sink into me, sink into the earth

From lust, make love, and from love, lust
demon and angel, heaven and hell;
God has always cursed the lovers
to chase
and even within each other, they chase —
see their bodies, catch them in between
their breaths turning hums turning songs
of worship, in rhythm with their rocks, forward,
back; a pliable chest and a hand by its heart, clutching as if
to grip the fluttering pulse and abduct her forever

The tempest of hell for the lustful,
caught up in its passion, that is wails and cries, but
often little kisses, spoiled by little laughter;
percussion drumming of flesh and spirit meeting,
drawing back, then thrusting into place again; the arc of
the devil's spine, the shudder of his legs, the spasm of
revolt against the angel who's taken his insides and
held him tight, tight by his belly, tighter, so clenched
he will soon tear from the virtue of this; the goodness,
the angel reminds him of goodness, long-forgotten,
replaced by the greed of the devil that says, Give me every drop of you,
give me even your blood, I've been soulless for too long,
and left emptied, needing to be whole again

Watch — the rain reveals itself and intermingles with the storm, but it comes
from within the first lovers, both unfolded and dripping to
come, hot, as the winds of their punishment are unmade with
the wet of maltreated, full lips, caught by open legs;
their bodies, still moving, to fight the finish, for eternity,
rebel against the loom of the end;
in their second circle of hell, they find
the opposite of death, between them:
life or creation or
merely joy

See, angels, that
everything will come in time,
and tomorrow there'll be new ways to love;
hear the devil and our chief prince, laughing,
Let all the lovers be jealous of us, they say,
they will never love like we do

HASHEM YIREH

Dorian Yosef Weber

<u>Content Warnings</u>: gender dysphoria, restraints, and a father nearly murdering his child

THE SUN WAS BRIGHT and the sky was clear as Yitzchak climbed Mount Moriah with his father. He hooked his thumbs into the straps holding wood to his back as he looked over the mountains and hills curving like a woman's hips.

"Son," Avraham said from behind Yitzchak, "come along. We have almost reached the peak."

Yitzchak turned to smile at his father. "Forgive me," he said. "Everything just looks so beautiful from up here."

Avraham hummed. "And it will look even more beautiful from the peak when we make an offering to our L-rd."

Yitzchak nodded and trotted along behind his father. Three days ago, his father had woken him before dawn had broken, frantically mumbling under his breath. *Father, what have you seen?* Yitzchak's father rarely talked about his life before Yitzchak had been born. All the boy knew of his father was that he was some sort of prophet who hoped to be the beginning of a long line of scholars who would study the weaving of the universe. Yitzchak, the first and only son, was a gift from G-d in his parents' elderly years and a means to that end. He had never told anyone the way the title felt like a skin stretched too tightly over a body holding more soul than it had room for.

We have to go. There is no time to tell your mother. The shock of it all would kill her. We have to leave and worship the L-rd on the peak of Mount Moriah.

Yitzchak's childhood had been spent being doted on by his parents as well as the hungry guests the two of them were constantly welcoming into their tents to eat and share their company. But none of them ever saw his parents when the fever of visions overcame their minds and they would speak frantically about what needed to be done but not why they needed to do it. It had frightened him as a child, but Yitzchak did not let it scare him anymore. He refused. If there was a twinge in his gut when his father shook him awake with blown-out pupils and matted hair, he would not acknowledge it and thus give it authority. He told himself that the uncomfortable knot had nothing to do with the way that he had silently and obediently followed along after his father and two of his men on a three-day journey. They did not take an animal to be sacrificed, but when Yitzchak had asked his father about what would be used, all he was told was that G-d would provide the sacrifice. Yitzchak was a good son; he always had been. It did not matter that the status of the eldest son was a weighted chain wrapped tight around his neck. He would not question the words of the L-rd or of his father.

Much of the trip up the mountain had been made in silence. Avraham had teased Yitzchak about women briefly, his voice and smile strained, and after Yitzchak had laughed and said that there had never been any he had been interested in, his father had just nodded jerkily and continued up the mountain. His mother, Sarah, had whispered once that the angels were terrifying, that seeing them rattled even the strongest of men. Whatever messenger had come to his father must have been holier than any other for the memory to cling to him so.

Content to leave his father to his higher, grander thoughts, Yitzchak began softly singing one of the hymns that Avraham had taught him. They sang them together, as a family, Yitzchak's voice soaring up alongside his mother's above the bassy vibrations rumbling out from his father's chest. They would sing over food and wine, teaching their songs to those passing through, and Yitzchak would fight to stay awake until the bleariness of a full stomach and whetted thirst made his eyelids heavy and he would fall asleep on the floor, head pillowed on his arms.

One night, when the three of them were alone, Yitzchak was curled up on the edge of sleep when, somewhere above him, whatever blurry conversation his parents had been having trailed off into silence. Yitzchak curiously winked one eye open but saw nothing but the wall of the tent. His parents were to his back.

"What troubles you?" his father asked in the soft, hoarse voice he saved only for his wife. Sarah was gasping shallowly, and it took a few seconds for Yitzchak to register that she was crying. "Why did the L-rd give us a child only for our bloodline to stop there?" Avraham sighed, and just from the sound of it Yitzchak could tell that they had had this conversation before. "It is not your fault."

"But it is no accident either!" Sarah snapped. "I love our son. I love him more than anything. I am happy with him and him alone. But a soul like his cannot find a wife or plant a seed in her womb. We have already grown old, and now we will die with no lineage but our soft, passive boy with the reborn soul of a sinning woman fixed in his chest. It must be my fault. I must have passed on a blemish that resides in my own spirit." Yitzchak realized that he was trembling, the wonder of hearing part of the truth lodged in his heart voiced aloud by the woman he loved most in the world sending quivering awe through his body.

Avraham hushed his wife. Yitzchak heard a shuffling and the whisper of fabric against fabric. They must have embraced each other.

"G-d will provide," Avraham whispered. "Have faith, and keep hold of the love that is in your heart. G-d listens to our prayers and will not forsake us."

"I'm just so lonely," Sarah sobbed. "I miss our families. I know we have left Avram and Sarai behind, and I love G-d and our flocks and the open sky and the way I can feel the seam where I have been stitched into everything else and it has been stitched into me. But I miss being like everyone else."

Avraham chuckled. "To be changed is not only to lose who you were before, but also to forget how to love what made that person who they were. I grieve Avram and Sarai every day, but every day I learn to love Avraham and Sarah and Yitzchak even more."

Sarah sighed. "Thank you," she said softly. A gentle hand began to stroke Yitzchak's hair, and he would know the touch of his mother anywhere.

He wished he had been able to say goodbye to her before he and his father had left for Moriah. Their household was filled with love, but Yitzchak and Sarah were special confidants. They understood each other and loved each other in a way that no one else could. It had only been three days, but Yitzchak already missed her terribly. He could not wait to see her again. The longing was an ache in his heart.

Before he could voice his pain aloud, Yitzchak followed his father around a lip of rock and, instead of more mountain, there was only rocky, flat ground. The air was thin in Yitzchak's lungs and, looking out across the landscape stretched out impossibly small like anthills and weeds, he finally realized how much closer to the heavens he had climbed.

He came up beside his father to join him, and the man's face was pale, too bloodless underneath the sweltering afternoon sun.

"Father?" Yitzchak asked. "Are you alright? Have you been visited by another messenger?"

Avraham shook his head. "All is well." The corners of his mouth twitched in an attempt to smile. "I am just too old to be climbing mountains. Let us set up the altar." Avraham arranged the firestone, and Yitzchak laid down the wood that he had carried on his back. Once the altar was finished, Yitzchak's father came up beside him and laid a hand on his shoulder. He turned to look up at him, smiling, and opened his mouth to ask about the sacrifice that the L-rd would provide. His voice died in his throat when he saw his father's solemn face.

Yitzchak's head began to shake of its own volition. "Father—"

Avraham had always been larger and stronger than Yitzchak. He made quick work of wrenching his wrists behind him and tying them together with a rough length of rope. Yitzchak tugged fruitlessly against it as his father wrapped his arms around him in one final embrace, the momentum of which he used to throw his son onto his back on top of the altar. Yitzchak's shoulders twinged as his arms were crushed underneath him.

His heart hammered in his chest. His father's clammy hand pressed down over top of his mouth, pinning him by clutching his skull too tightly for Yitzchak to be able to move it. He screamed against his stone-faced father's palm loud enough for his voice to crack and fray at the edges. The sacrificial knife glinted in Avraham's free hand. As Yitzchak helplessly kicked his legs, he realized that he had soiled himself.

He was looking up at his father, but also he was standing several feet away, watching his own body thrash like a frenzied prey animal. As his father slowly raised up the knife, what felt like rain dropped against Yitzchak's eyelids. He blinked it away, and when he opened his eyes again there was another figure looming above him.

The world around Yitzchak was already so bright and loud, so the stranger's brilliance was too much to comprehend. There were only flashes of hands and wings and hooves and eyes, so many eyes, all of them weeping. Their tears mingled with Yitzchak's own, gravity pulling them down to the back of the sockets, ready to eat away at the nerves.

Avraham's grip had loosened, his hand shaking and spasming, but Yitzchak had stopped fighting. He just lay there limply. He was the firstborn son of a prophet. He would be a good son. It was his duty to bear this weight that had always felt like it was meant for someone else. It was his duty to bear it, to let everyone believe that he was the man that would usher in countless generations with strength and dignity.

"Please," he whispered to his father in a hoarse, high voice, higher than that of any man he had ever met, something that he savored even now. "When you tell mother, keep her away from the wells and the cliffs. Tell her that I love her, and that I did not struggle." The latter was a lie, but one that Yitzchak hoped might save his mother's life.

Avraham did not answer, he only raised the knife higher. Yitzchak watched him do it from over Avraham's shoulder.

"Avraham," the stranger said in countless quivering voices. Yitzchak dimly realized that he was finally seeing one of his father's angels. It wasn't terrifying like his mother had claimed it to be. It was beautiful. It touched Yitzchak's face gently, and he nuzzled against the warm softness of it. His father did not heed the call, and Yitzchak watched and waited for the knife in his throat.

"Avraham!" the angel called again, louder and more urgent, and Avraham's head finally jerked up to look at it.

"Here I am," he whispered, his gaze far away.

"Do not raise your hand against the boy," the angel said, "or do anything to him. For now I know that you fear G-d, since you have not withheld your son, your favored one, from Me." Yitzchak could feel it watching not his body on the altar, but the version of him standing beyond it.

Avraham's grip went slack around the knife, and it fell to the ground with a thud. His gaze wandered to the right, and he staggered off to investigate something out of Yitzchak's sight. He watched his body roll off the altar and fall to the ground, throwing up a cloud of dust as he gagged and gasped and retched. Then the angel was in front of him.

"You were trapped in there for much too long," it said kindly. "Come along with me, I will show you the place that has been made for you."

One of Yitzchak's souls watched his body, the form that had never been his. The other curled up into a ball and sobbed.

"I think you have the wrong one," said the Yitzchak calmly standing on his feet. "I am the firstborn son. I am the one whom the knife was meant for."

"And it found you," the angel responded. "This body was never yours, it was only a vessel you were stuffed into alongside that other spirit. I will bring you home." The soul that was no longer Yitzchak did not respond. He stood silently and watched his companion cry.

"Do not fear," the angel said. "You will see her again."

"I will trust in the L-rd," the soul finally said, finding peace in the words as he spoke them. "I will go with you."

"Thank you," the angel said, and then Yitzchak was alone.

Avraham came back to the altar with a ram, lustrous and without blemish. Yitzchak watched him mechanically sacrifice it with dull eyes. Once the deed was done, Avraham turned and shuffled off to begin making his way down the mountain, mumbling to an angel that Yitzchak could not hear.

As Avraham slowly departed from the altar, Yitzchak sat up with trembling, weak arms. The rope had come untied as a result of either angelic intervention or lucky coincidence, and Yitzchak, now freed, sat back against the blood-slick altar. The landscape was just as beautiful as it had been minutes ago, but it sat differently in Yitzchak's chest now. It felt lighter, more free. Now that the other one was gone, Yitzchak could feel the place where the two souls had been chafing against each other. The burning of it was gone, in its place nothing but a soothing wholeness.

Yitzchak braced her forearms on the altar and heaved herself to her feet. She took a moment to drink in the land sprawling below her and listen to the soft sounds of the wind and the birds. Then, she followed her father down the slopes of Mount Moriah.

PIECES

Emily Hoffman

<u>Content Warnings</u>: gore

SOMETIMES KIERAN WONDERED if he could pinpoint it. If thinking hard enough would allow him to select a specific moment – or at least a specific day – when the last bits of his humanity had slipped away. When the cold bodies in front of him had ceased being people and had become parts with price tags. Things to be divided up, bagged, and stuffed into boxes in a giant, industrial, walk-in freezer.

It had reminded him of Costco, at first. Overstuffed, and frigid. Except instead of bulk produce, and dried goods, there were boxes of heads. Arms. Torsos. Spines with shoulders, and spines without. He'd canceled his Costco membership a week after he'd started working. Hadn't stepped foot in one for years.

Maybe that had been the day – the day when he'd finally gone back. When the gigantic freezers at the store had stopped sending a shiver down his spine, and it had all become relative. When boxes of heads were suddenly no different than boxes of grapes.

His mother would have been disappointed.

Not that it mattered, he'd disappointed her years ago. She'd been so pleased when he'd gone into medicine instead of opera. Her odd, dramatic little boy finally choosing the respectable path. Maybe if she'd known where his career had been headed, she wouldn't have made such a fuss over his boyfriends. How immoral could dating men be when you divided body parts up like a butcher, and sold them off for a living?

He did his best to shake those thoughts off. To keep them from lingering. To keep from making any moral judgements against himself. This wasn't murder, it was business. Nothing more, nothing less. He wondered sometimes if he'd have felt better working during the day, when the building felt more like an office. When it was populated, and there was a receptionist out front, smiling and answering phones. When there was light outside, and they could all pretend they didn't do work that was truly morbid. He'd appreciated the ability to hide behind pleasantries for a few weeks, but eventually the feeling had faded. It felt false. Like a lie strung together to appease someone he couldn't identify. No one living – save for those employed there – would ever see past the front desk, so perhaps the facade was simply for the dead. A small prayer to already departed souls that they not return to haunt here. Something about that seemed even more distasteful to Kieran.

Either the souls were gone, or they weren't. If they were present enough to care about what happened to their bodies after death, then perhaps this wasn't the sort of business anyone should partake in. No one had ever taken home a ghost, though. And there was nothing that roamed the halls after dark. So Kieran had felt safe to discard the pleasantries. To do his work unbothered, when no one else could see.

There was less judgment, in the middle of the night, even if it lacked sunshine and smiles.

He'd developed a routine over the last few years. Arrive at 10:00pm, turn the lights on, check his cut sheets. Turn on something operatic as loud as the music would go, and then work until morning. It felt better, somehow, stepping out into the morning light than it did to leave in the evening. Maybe he was more worried about ghosts than he actually cared to admit. Not that he'd ever speak such a thing out loud.

It should have been a normal night. Normal enough, anyway, if you were misfortunate enough to consider segmenting bodies up throughout the evening to be normal. He barely heard the knocks at the front door between his music and the bone saw, chewing its way through cold sinew, and marrow. The sound hardly cut through to the back hallways in the first place, it felt like divine intervention — that one of the raps against glass would occur during a momentary lull in the ongoing noise.

He'd never considered himself a brave man, despite the iron stomach he seemed to have when dealing exclusively with the dead. And answering the front door of a tissue bank in the middle of the night was high on his list of things not to do — certainly not while he was by himself. Tissue — bodies — sold for more than he felt comfortable considering. Thousands of dollars, depending on the piece. Then again, body snatchers hardly seemed like the sorts to knock, given the criminality of the whole escapade.

So he waited.

Stilled.

Held his breath until the knock came again, three short raps against glass, followed by a muffled sound that echoed down the halls behind it. Like a voice. A deep sort of bass that he felt in his chest, bones vibrating under his skin, despite the fact that he couldn't actually claim to have *heard* anything.

Right then.

The process of making himself fit to answer the door was an arduous one. Gloves were removed. His face mask. His apron. Scrubs were checked over for spots of blood, and his hands were washed. He'd hoped that the knocking would end in the interim — it didn't. The voice called again. It was definitely a voice, he'd decided, rumbling down the hallway like music from a club a block away.

" — hold on — "

It didn't make sense to respond really, no one could hear him from the back. He muttered the words regardless, heaving a sigh as he wound his way to the front office. His nerves tingled, trilling under his skin like they'd decided all on their own that he needed to run. And he felt like a child, suddenly, sprinting up the basement stairs at night so whatever lurked in the dark couldn't catch him. He couldn't quite temper the feeling, so he found himself speeding up — steps only slowing once the office doors came into view.

For a split second he wondered if he'd fallen asleep, somehow. If he was dreaming, or if he'd lost time. Or if, perhaps, the night had just flown past him — because it was bright out. Just for a moment. Bright enough for him to mistake the middle of the night for dawn breaking. And there were prisms behind the glass. Bright, shifting rainbows. Confusing for all of a minute until they shifted into the shape of a man, lanky, and hovering in the darkness.

A man who suddenly knocked at the glass again, pulling Kieran back into himself.

He was tall. That was about all that Kieran could make out through the doors. Tall, and angular, leaning like a Ken Doll being operated by a toddler. Kieran blinked awkwardly, nose wrinkling as he scrambled for the door to open it before the man could knock again. " –Can I help you?"

It would have sounded rude, had he been in a customer service position of any kind. As it stood, he wasn't exactly used to talking to anyone other than himself during working hours. The man blinked back, ducking some as he made an attempt to shift into what little light there was. "You sell bodies here, yes? Pieces of them? Cut them off and sell them for ... science?"

Kieran frowned, and his dumbfounded silence stretched out for a too long minute.

"Science." The man repeated the word like he'd only just learned it yesterday and it still felt wrong in his mouth. His head shook as if he somehow disapproved of the entire thought. "I need something removed and sold. Can you do that for me?"

Kieran blinked again, eyebrows furrowing. " – I don't know what you think we do here, but it's not ... that."

The other man's eyebrows furrowed, like he'd never made the movement himself before, but instinctively felt the need to echo Kieran's expression. "This is a tissue bank, is it not? That's what I was told. You remove pieces from people and sell them."

"Well ... yes." Kieran blinked. "But those people are dead, we take .... We take donated tissue and divide it up. Then it gets shipped out for research. This isn't some sort of body modification ... operation." He paused, frown flickering across his face. "I don't know what your deal is, but I think you probably need help that I'm not capable of giving —" He shrugged, stepping back to close the door. There was work to do. Work that had nothing to do with the very clearly unhinged man outside.

"I need my wings cut off. Please. I don't ask this lightly, and I would not be in front of you now if I did not find this necessary." Well. Damn. Kieran paused, if only because the offered explanation was so unexpected that it ground him to a halt. "My name is Wyatt. It is not the name I was given, it is just the name that I like. And I need your help, please." Wyatt blinked, reaching to curl slender fingers around the door before he gently pulled it open again. "I understand that this might be difficult to process, would it help if I showed you? My wings, I mean."

" ... No." It was the only thing Kieran could think to say. The only English word that came to mind in the silence that followed Wyatt's question. "No, I think I'm okay, I think I should go, I have work — I have work to do."

"Please wait —" Kieran shook his head, even as Wyatt stepped away from the door and shed his jacket like it was a second skin.

Lock the door.

Step away.

Go back to work.

Call the police if he doesn't leave —

" — I'll call the police, I will." The words fell from his mouth like an echo from an unfamiliar part of his brain. The part that took over when every other bit was occupied elsewhere, watching Wyatt awkwardly work at the buttons of his shirt like it somehow impossibly contained the wings he'd promised to show off. "Are you listening to me? Stop —"

Bile rose in the back of his throat. Anxiety swelling up from his stomach in the form of acid. And he couldn't even pinpoint why. Maybe the other man was crazy, but he seemed harmless. Kieran lived in a city, he had for years. He'd seen worse than this on the public bus system on more than one occasion. But this felt different. It made his skin tingle. It threw him right back to his youth, into that fear that crept up in the middle of the night.

What if he was about to look at something people shouldn't see?

What if Hell was real?

What if this was the straw that broke the camel's back and condemned him?

What if all those priests had been right?

"Please stop. Please. I don't want to know, I don't want to be involved —" There was no use to it. The words barely made their way out before Wyatt's shirt fluttered to the ground and the world fractured. Kieran was used to bodies. To parts. To the little bits and bobs that made up a person. He'd gone numb to it over time. People were all the same, at the end of the day. Heads, fingers, arms, shoulders. They cut the same way. Separated from the body the same way. Tissue, muscle, then bone. This was ... "What the fuck —"

"I am sorry. If it's jarring, I know it can be jarring ...." Wyatt frowned, lips pressing together as the wind gently fluttered through outstretched feathers. He reached back out to the door, re-opening it as Kieran stiffened, and stepped through. "Now that you can see them, can you help me? Please?"

There was an innocence to the question that didn't carry any of the weight it actually involved. The weight of what Wyatt was asking for. Like he'd strolled in, in the middle of the night, simply lost and asking for direction. Like he hadn't overturned Kieran's entire worldview just by showing up at the door.

"Are you fucking kidding me?"

"Are you asking if I'm telling a joke?" Wyatt frowned. "Why would I do that?" Another pause lingered before Wyatt took a breath, wings bristling behind him. It felt like a hallucination. Like some kind of uncanny valley nightmare, CGI come to life in an all too realistic fashion. "This is the right place of business, yes? You call yourself a body broker –"

"No," Kieran interrupted, nearly choking on the word. He'd never loved the term, really. Body broker. It felt like a job title from some kind of futuristic hellscape. It was why he'd never involved himself in the business end of things. He didn't deal with the selling, or obtaining. He just dealt with the parts. He'd been able to separate himself from the rest of it. Maybe that was his problem now. He'd managed to drain the humanity from all of it. He collected them. Sorted the pieces. Made sure the cuts were precise, and the labels.

Someone else dealt with the selling. With their final destination. He supposed the pieces all went to labs. To scientists. To researchers. That's how he'd been able to stomach it. People were just electricity contained in a body, and when the lights went out – he divided up the parts and sent them onward, so maybe other people's lights could stay on longer. If there was no such thing as a soul, it didn't matter what happened to the body after death. It wasn't like anyone was watching.

Except now he was staring down an angel.

And that angel wanted his wings removed.

"I deal with dead people, not live — " He paused, clearing his throat. "Not ... anything living. I'm not in the business of body modification, and I don't just sell parts off. I wouldn't even know who to contact, especially not about —" His voice trailed off as he gestured weakly towards Wyatt, and the feathered wings that towered behind him.

Jesus.

That had to be some kind of mutation. Or make-up. Maybe it was some kind of contraption he had strapped on and this was all some sort of hidden camera joke.

"I'll deal with selling them. I just need you to remove them." Wyatt seemed calm. Especially given the circumstances. His face was still. Good natured despite the inherent violence he was asking Kieran to commit.

"Okay, let's say they are real —" Kieran sighed, scrubbing at his face.

"They are." Wyatt only stared, wings stretching in response. "Touch them, you'll see —"

"I don't want — I don't want to touch them." Kieran grimaced, jaw clenching as he backed a step up, like the space would somehow give him the distance he needed to click his reality back into place. It didn't. It made it worse, somehow, giving him a full view. " — Even if they are real, I can't — I work with dead people, not live ones. I don't have bandages, or painkillers —"

"Pain is part of what makes someone human, I have no wish to numb it." Wyatt blinked, eyebrows furrowing as he took a step forward. Christ, of course he sounded like some kind of psalm. "Please. If you don't take them from me, one of my brothers will, and they won't show nearly the care. I've seen it happen. I've done it. You have no idea what it's like, to have something ripped from you by someone you love. They don't care for clean cuts, they tear. The scar is the point. It's a punishment —"

"Why would you need to be punished?" Kieran stepped away again, back hitting the receptionist's desk and jarring him back into some sense of reality.

"Because humans are curious beings. And when I found curiosity, I also found fear. And then it all came flooding in like a plague, and those feelings aren't for us, they're for you." Wyatt glowered as he held out his hand. "If you need to touch them to convince yourself, please do."

"I don't want to." Kieran's lips pressed into a line as he leaned backwards. It was too much, all of it. The talk of angels and punishments. "When I was little, my mother — my mother read me that psalm about how it's harder for a camel to get through the eye of a needle than it is for someone to get into heaven. And I used to lie awake at night paralyzed by it, because — well, then it had to be impossible, and that never made sense. I mean, how could God love us and still make it so hard, and if we were all going to hell anyway, then what was the point? Why put us here to suffer, and then suffer some more?" The words spilled out like thread unspooling from a tightly packed bobbin. He nearly choked on them. He'd shoved them down for so long, those thoughts had long since faded away.

God wasn't real.

Bodies were just flesh animated by electricity.

And here he was talking to an angel.

"She read the psalm incorrectly. It's harder for a rich man to get into heaven than it is for a camel to get through the eye of a needle. And the eye of a needle is simply a structure on earth. In what you call Israel. It's tall. Camels are perfectly capable of squeezing through as long as they duck." Wyatt nodded, stepping closer again until he could take Kieran's hand. It would have been funny, had Kieran not been so shell shocked.

"You don't understand, I gave up — I gave up on all of it, and now I've done so much wrong — and I've cut so many bodies into pieces, and I'm — I can't put this on my list too. You cut up an angel, that has to be a shot straight to hell, right? Do not pass go, do not collect $200."

Wyatt frowned, head cocking to the side as Kieran spoke. "I don't understand that phrase –"

"You don't need to." Kieran shook his head in response, fingers moving of their own volition to stroke through feathers just barely within reach.

Fuck.

Fuck.

Of course they were warm. And of course they felt safe, and somehow electrified. And very, very fucking real.

"I won't let you go to hell, Kieran. I promise. You do this for me and you'll fear for nothing." Wyatt nodded, breath held as he watched Kieran's face shift into something softer.

"How could you promise something like that?" Kieran countered, despite the fact that his resolve was steadily crumbling the closer he stepped. The longer his fingers grazed Wyatt's feathers.

"I would not say it if I did not mean it ..."

A long pause lingered, as Kieran took another breath, withdrawing his hand only to nod down the hallway. Maybe this was all just a dream anyway. Some kind of vivid nightmare. And whether it was, or it wasn't — perhaps it was best just to end it. "It's going to hurt no matter what I do." He sighed, glancing at the angel behind him as he wound through the hallways. There was a first aid kit along the way. It wouldn't help much, but some bandaging was better than nothing, he supposed.

"I know." Wyatt's answer was so simple that Kieran nearly paused in the hallway. Just to ask again why any of this was necessary. Why his resolve was so set. Why he would be so fearful of family he loved that he'd seek out a stranger to wound him instead.

"You're sure? That you want them gone?" Kieran paused at the doorway to his makeshift morgue. It all seemed colder than before, somehow. Bright and upsetting like an acid trip gone wildly wrong. Like the body parts he'd wrapped and set aside could spring back to life at any moment. Perhaps they could, all things considered.

"I'm sure." Wyatt nodded, pressing past Kieran into the room ahead. He seemed more angelic, somehow, in the middle of the space. When there weren't shadows hiding his lack of imperfections. Kieran found himself holding his breath. It felt wrong. It made his stomach churn. Like he was about to hack the head off of a Greek statue.

"I'll try my best to bandage it, but it's going to bleed no matter what I do...." The words were more for himself than for Wyatt, really. An attempt to keep himself calm. Like this was business as usual, somehow. Just cut off the pieces and move on to the next body. He could do that, couldn't he? He did that every day. It would help, if he fell back into his routine. Opera, gloves, apron, bone saw.

Except there was no checklist, now. No cut sheet. No guide to follow. Just Wyatt, standing with his wings outstretched and waiting. It was louder than normal, the bone saw. Jarring in the middle of the silence that surrounded them. Kieran reached out, touching Wyatt's back. Well – the wings were definitely attached.

Connected to flesh between his shoulder blades like a monstrous kind of bird.

He didn't offer a countdown, he couldn't.

If he hesitated any longer, they'd be there until morning.

He just needed to cut, like always.

Metal though flesh, then muscle, then bone. Muscle, and bone, and so much blood. The crunch of it all had never bothered him before. The grinding of metal teeth through marrow. The grind, and the thud of a heavy, dead wing hitting the floor.

If God hadn't loved him before, he never would now.

He felt that in the pit of his stomach, even as he continued.

Then again, maybe it was all just pieces. Maybe wings were just pieces too. Maybe this was all he'd been meant to do.

PARADISES

Rafael Nicolás

<u>Content Warnings</u>: graphic sex, referenced abuse

THE ANGEL GABRIEL travels to the temple of Tlāloc, one night, and he confesses his love. He falls, kneeling, before the God of Rain, and he puts his hands together, interlocks the fingers.

He says, "Lord, after I tucked my Father into bed, I ran to my room, and I found my best clothes." On the angel, there's just an alb, lace stitched along the bottom, down from knees to ankles, with thin string pulled into a bow by the dip of his sweet neck. "While he slept, I snuck from the house, I ran through his Eden garden, and I flew past the gates of heaven." Bowing his head, he trembles. "And now I'm here, before you, in your own paradise."

"And why," says the god, "have you come?" On his throne, Tlāloc is enormous — the size of a sun, while Gabriel is a measly star, distant, half in stature and bright. "Only the souls I drown are welcome here, and you're but a child."

"I'm not a child!" Gabriel cries, raising his head, meeting the gaze of the great being, who is blue-faced, fanged, and tough as the stone that his temples are built of on earth. "I'm more ancient than the universe, and too long I've been called nothing more than the child of my Father—"

Tlāloc interrupts: "But why have you come?"

"You—You—" Gabriel stammers, his eyebrows tugging together, his own mouth twitching, as he wonders if the God of Rain had forgotten. "You invited me." The gesture of prayer leaves his hands; he raises one, waves it with the emphasis of his words. "You came into my Father's house, not more than a century ago, and you asked if I could love, and when you were told I couldn't, you said that if I ever changed, I was welcome in your temple." He swallows the razor of anxiety on his tongue; he adds, "I've always loved. I've really always loved too much. I stayed by my Father when his first child left, and I stood with him as my other siblings each began to leave him one by one. And, now, it's just him and I. Him, making new earths every week, forgetting them and their people; then me, helping him to bed on the seventh days and bringing a spoon of soup to his mouth each dawn."

Tlāloc lifts his god body, stands giant not far from the beautiful angel with too many wings sprouting from him, like a seed unsure which direction to grow. "And now you leave your senile Father too?"

"I'll return," Gabriel promises, lifting his chin to meet the all-encompassing white of Tlāloc's eyes. "I'll return so soon, he'll never have noticed I was ever gone. It's not right to leave someone so frail all by himself. But when I go back to him, I won't be a child anymore, not an angel." When the all-powerful tells him to stand, Gabriel listens, stumbling but rising nonetheless. "I've always loved too much. I loved him. I forgave him for whatever the others said he did."

"I knew it was a lie," Tlāloc admits, "when your Father told me you couldn't love."

Off-handedly, Gabriel replies, "My Father told me that it was my sibling Lucifer who is the king of lies."

"Like mother," Tlāloc jokes, "like daughter." He extends a hand that Gabriel reaches for, only to find, in comparison, his palm and fingers puny and delicate, asking to be broken apart. "But I think he was only trying to protect you, angel."

Gabriel would reply that he doesn't want to be called an angel any longer, but he knows this to be the final moment that it's true, so he accepts the name, cherishes it for the last time. "Your last wife — she was kidnapped from you; she was the jewel of your paradise, but she was stolen, then dug into the soil, and she budded from the ground as a flower, and she became the god Xōchipilli. He didn't forgive you; he said he had no interest in being your wife anymore because you didn't know love." Tlāloc's other hand rises to the jaw of the angel, cradles him there. "And then your second wife, Chalchiuhtlicue, you loved too much. You kissed her body until it began to water down, and she dripped down from this heaven, and she became the lakes of the earth."

Tlāloc muses, "I had only recently lost her, when I asked your Father of you." He cranes his head down to him — there are the rattles, like those of serpents — and his breath is cold, like the breeze of a hurricane. "Will I love you too little or too much?"

"Any love at all," Gabriel sighs, "is enough for me. I'll meet you where you are." Tlāloc takes his mouth, but nothing more than a press forward, slow, then pulls back. He murmurs, "I'm sorry that I couldn't dress nicer for you. My Father has never let me own too many things. If I could, I would have put flowers in my hair and beads around my neck. I would have painted my face in the yellow your wives wore, and I would have put silver through my nose."

"I can dress you," Tlāloc replied, "in all the jade of the earth."

The kiss that follows is deeper, pushing whereas Tlāloc's arms are pulling Gabriel close by the waist, tugging him upward so that he can love his mouth comfortably. Gabriel wonders if he'll become larger from this, if he'll swell to the size of a universe, become like a god already; and he opens his mouth, allows Tlāloc to explore the tongue that's never known more than the fruit and seed of a garden. The god seizes it, thrusting in his own tongue, then gripping Gabriel tighter by the hip bones that the angel worries will crack beneath the jagged strength. But, he doesn't fight, presses needy, up against a deity he's always thought to be frightening and lovely at once.

Tlāloc's fangs graze Gabriel's plump lips, and if the angel could bleed, he knew he'd be spilling onto his white tunic, staining her, staining himself. He whines, high in a way he never has before, and then he feels the god walk toward the throne, realizes his eyes had shut, and he feels a ripple startle his body. Then, he feels the hardness of a throne's seat, against his back. Tlāloc pulls away, looks down at Gabriel, and Gabriel stares up at him, feeling small but knowing it won't be for much longer. He's happy, he thinks, as Tlāloc hitches his alb far up to his waist, revealing the in-between of his legs. Divinity burrowed there, jutting out from there.

Tlāloc is in a cloak, weaved with more colors than there are words for, the same as there is in the complex tie at his groin, hiding him. With one hand, he undoes it, and he shows himself to Gabriel, as if to ask if this is alright, and Gabriel doesn't reply, but he parts his legs, plants his feet by the edge of the seat he lies upon. Not long after, Tlāloc takes his ankles, however, raises them so that Gabriel now feels too exposed to the wetness of the Rain God's paradise.

He asks, before it's too late, "Can I have another kiss?" Tlāloc, eagerly, gives it to him — his lips are damp, contain all the downpour of the earth on them. "And," he adds, this time against the mouth of the god, "will you let me live here, with you?"

Tlāloc, instead of answering, leans into Gabriel, pressing in, slipping into the tight hold of the warm angel, who jerks and flinches. But the push is careful, delicate, and Gabriel breathes out, so slow and long, he believes his soul is leaving, and he's becoming something else. More than spirit, more than even his god. He's happy to be kissed again; their lips clash with a little playfulness, smacking and pulling, teasing each other to move. Gabriel kicks out a leg, tries to strike Tlāloc with it so that he'll surge ahead to take him. There's a part of the angel that fears his Father will wake before the deed is done, and he'll barge into the temple, and grab his last child by the hair and drag him back to the empty heaven surrounded by an empty garden.

Gabriel sings as Tlāloc begins to rock forward, pushing in deeper than Gabriel knew his body extended. He can feel the god from where he entered him, up even past his belly, out his mouth, in his head, in his heart, in his hands. He tries to pull the other closer, wanting to be held, and Tlāloc obliges, losing the grip on Gabriel's ankles to wrap his arms all around him, ruffling the feathers of wings splayed out beneath him. In return, Gabriel continues his little song, though it's breathy and trembling with the weight of this — these quick, loud strikes into him, like thunder. Tlāloc, too, is the God of Storms; Gabriel remembers only vaguely.

Tlāloc, not long after, raises the angel, twists them both, though without daring to pull out from him; the god returns to his seat on the throne, the angel placed on his lap. Gabriel doesn't mind, his hips shuddering in place before they nervously rise, lower. Flying, falling. Tlāloc is allowing him to lead, and Gabriel tries to keep up, as if to prove his worth. The sea of his hair, as if caught by wind, tussles and flails, as Tlāloc runs his hands all over him, squeezing, rubbing, groping tight. When he begins to thrust his own hips up into Gabriel, the angel moves opposite to him, meeting the god's every attack with his own. Finally, Tlāloc silences Gabriel's psalms with another kiss.

The first time, Gabriel reels back and cries loud, his entire body shaking, unfamiliar with the sensation of love he's been taught never to have. All his wings stretch and flutter, he feels heat on him, and then, in him. His eyes are overcome with stars, stars that he thinks, momentarily, to be the culprit of the raging fever on his body. From his mouth, a soft, tender whisper, a beg, to be loved another time. Tlāloc lifts him, and then he travels with him, like before, but he brings him into a bedroom, where he places Gabriel over the raised mat, and then he throws himself over him again, has him again. Gabriel begs him never to stop, that he wants to do this for eternity, he'll spend the rest of his infinite days here, he says. And it was so — for longer than a human can understand — that they were caught in a haze of love-making that Gabriel almost forgot that he'd ever been an angel. He only thinks of the new clothes he'll don, and the new name he'll adopt, as the consort of the God of Rain.

He's not sure what kind of god he'll be, but maybe he doesn't need to decide. His Father never had, or maybe he'd forgotten if he ever had a purpose. Gabriel thinks that there's so little that elderly man remembers now.

Exhaustion wears the gods out, but only after so many suns have risen and fallen that Gabriel has lost count. They collapse entangled onto the bed, in another haze, a different fog of love, and they kiss again, but lazily. Even now, they haven't grown tired of touching each other, and Gabriel thinks that maybe they never will, and he smiles and kisses each jewel engraved on the face of his husband.

He mumbles, "I will never leave you. I belong to you now. And you belong to me. If I'm without you, I'll go dry like a river and all the plants that drink from me will wither."

Tlāloc brings his head to Gabriel's chest, and he mumbles against him, "You said you would return to your Father, after this. Have you changed your mind, my love?" One of his hands goes to Gabriel's hip, skims to his waist, his belly, pats him there.

Distantly, Gabriel smiles, though he worries. "Do you have any empty rooms in your paradise?"

"There are too many to count, but if you need even more, I'll have all the spirits of my paradise build another hundred, another thousand."

"I'd like to bring my Father here," Gabriel states, putting his own hand over

Tlāloc's. "He'll have no choice. He doesn't know how to care for himself. He's so old, and if he's dying, then I want his last days to be in this paradise of yours that's true and beautiful and kinder." He hesitates. "But maybe coming here, seeing you and I, will make him remember to live again. I hope that he remembers love, too, at least for his children. I love him too much, you see. I always have."

CONTRIBUTORS

Tyler Battaglia is a queer and disabled horror and dark fantasy author. He is interested in the intersections of monsters and horror with queerness and disability. Tyler lives in Ottawa, Canada, with his partner and their grumpy cat. He can be found on Twitter at @whosthistyler, hosting the prompt event #Saturdark. Find more at www.tylerbattaglia.com.

Morgan Dante is the author of the MMF paranormal romance novella *A Flame In The Night*. They have a soft spot for all things dark and gothic, especially vampires and an array of castle-dwelling monsters. They've never written an angel that they didn't want to make at least a little weird-looking.

Daniel Marie James is a trans artist with a BA in Creative Writing and MFA in Book Art from Mills College. While he typically focuses on his long-form novels, he occasionally writes poetry focusing on trauma, and processing trauma through art.

Ian Haramaki is a gay, trans, and mixed Japanese author of fantasy, romance, and historical fiction based out of Colorado. He enjoys making fictional men kiss and living life as a tanuki. Most of his time is spent peddling dinosaur merchandise to nerds at fan conventions. His Twitter is @cometkins.

Emily Hoffman is an actor, writer, and was once described as a 'cryptid enthusiast' by TMZ and Newsweek. She holds a degree in theatre and playwrighting, and can commonly be found giving haunted pub tours or running scavenger hunts though Pike Place Market. She's pleased to have found her way back to writing, and to be included in a publication with such outstanding people.

Quinton Li (they/them) is a Melbourne-based non-binary novelist, poet and fiction editor. Their debut novel, *Tell Me How It Ends*, is a cozy coming-of-age fantasy novel with a queer & diverse cast, tarot cards and witches. Their poetry can be found with *Panorame Press*, *Messy Misfits Club* and *Iris Youth Magazine*. Find more at quintonli.com.

Aurélio Loren is a queer, disabled author who focuses on the intersection of queerness and horror. The grotesque, the chilling, and the ominous are all things that can be found in his work. They are on Twitter at @swampeddddd.

Freydís Moon (they/él/ella) is an internationally bestselling author, diviner, poet, and creator, writing love stories in the Fantasy, Horror, and Speculative categories. Fond of culture, mysticism, history, and language, they constantly find themself lost in a book, trying their hand at a new recipe, or planning a trip to a faraway place.

Rafael Nicolás is the author of *Angels Before Man* (2023) and other queer fiction. He likes being gay.

Rae Novotny (any pronouns) is a novelist, angel liker, and spec fic sucker from the U.S. South. She is best known for posting infrequent illustrations of man tits on Twitter @ fathommore.

Alex Patrascu is a graphic designer who accidentally learned about words. When not snacking on sans serif fonts, she can be found reading a copious amount of books or drawing art of the various characters that haunt her mind. Check out her work at apatrascu.com.

Angela Sun is a writer with an interest in the ugly and the divine. Her poetry can be found in *Squawk Back, Heavy Feather Review*, and "Summer Gothic" by *Panorame Press*. She can be found on twitter as @blessphemey.

Cas Trudeau is a graduate of Carnegie Mellon University with a MA in Literary and Cultural Studies. Their writing explores the symbolization of memory, the joy of gender enfleshment, and queerness in southern settings.

When he's not outside hunting for trinkets and foraging for snacks, **Dorian Yosef Weber** writes adult fiction at the intersections of his queerness, disability, and Jewish identity. He is particularly passionate about creating representation in fiction of his Orthodox siblings and depicting disabled and queer trauma, fight, love, and home.

REPRINT

Angel at Harvest Church originally appears in https://freydismoon.medium.com/on-a-sweltering-sunday-morning-an-angel-hollers-versus-from-behind-a-sturdy-pulpit-your-father-5a4632c4a112

Printed in Great Britain
by Amazon